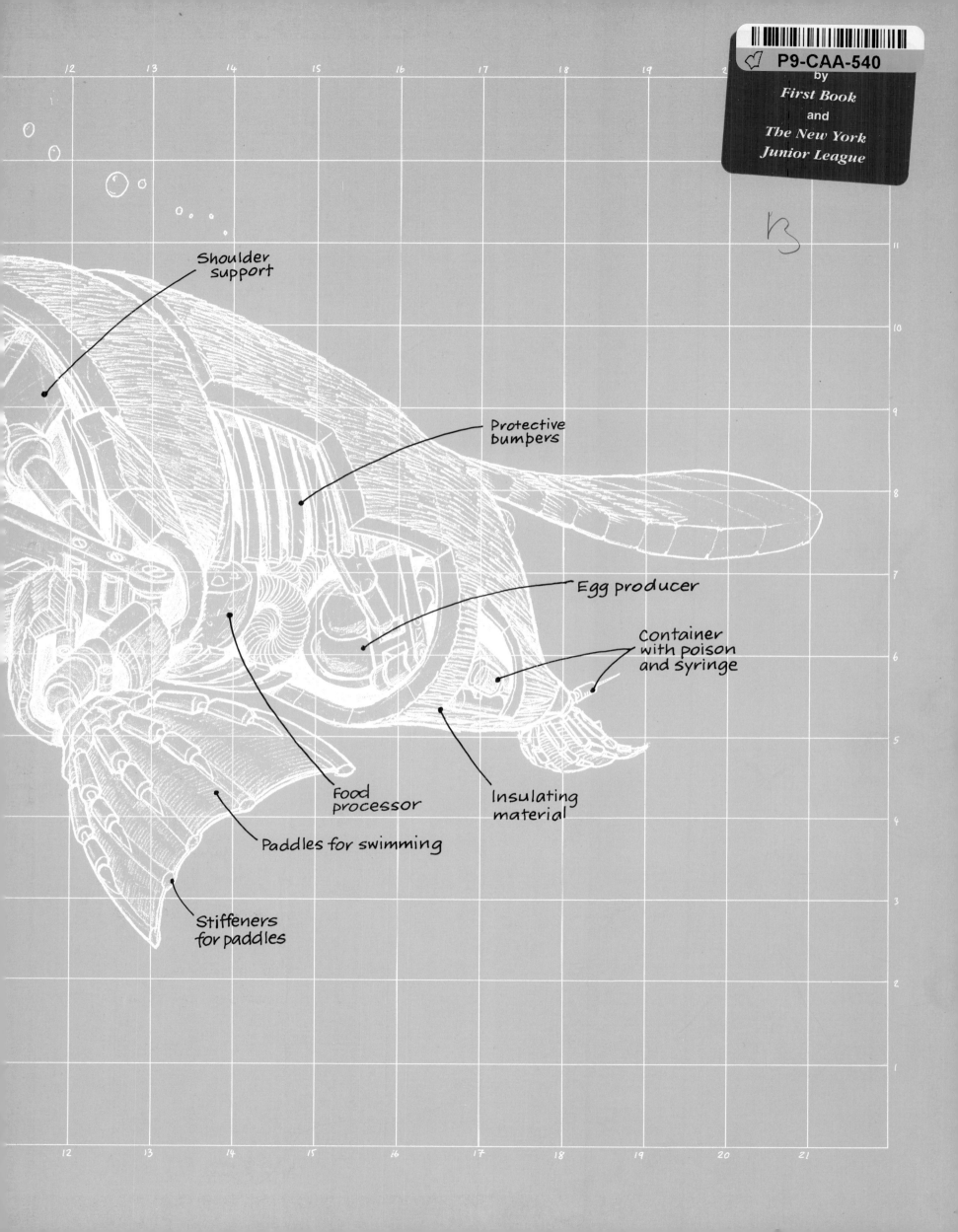

Shoulder
support

Protective
bumpers

Egg producer

Container
with poison
and syringe

Food
processor

Insulating
material

Paddles for swimming

Stiffeners
for paddles

A Marshall Edition
Conceived, edited, and designed by Marshall Editions,
170 Piccadilly, London W1V 9DD

First published in the U.S.A. in 1994 by
Turner Publishing, Inc.
A Subsidiary of Turner Broadcasting System, Inc.
1050 Techwood Drive, N.W.
Atlanta, Georgia 30318

10 9 8 7 6 5 4 3 2 1

Distributed by Andrews and McMeel
A Universal Press Syndicate Company
4900 Main Street
Kansas City, Missouri 64112

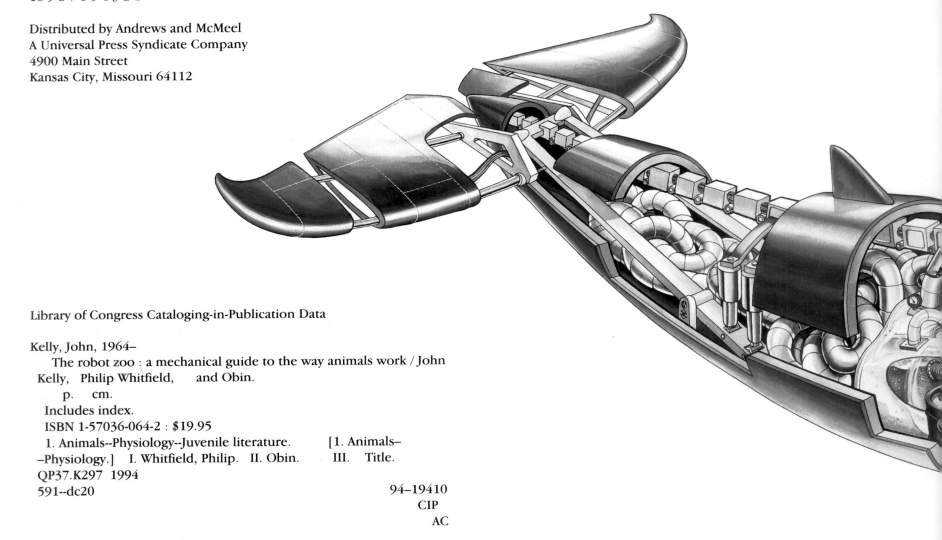

Library of Congress Cataloging-in-Publication Data

Kelly, John, 1964–
    The robot zoo : a mechanical guide to the way animals work / John
Kelly,   Philip Whitfield,   and Obin.
        p.   cm.
    Includes index.
    ISBN 1-57036-064-2 : $19.95
    1. Animals--Physiology--Juvenile literature.   [1. Animals–
–Physiology.]   I. Whitfield, Philip. II. Obin.   III.   Title.
QP37.K297 1994
591--dc20   94–19410
                                                                    CIP
                                                                     AC

Executive editor: Cynthia O'Brien
Project editor: Kate Scarborough
Art Director: Branka Surla
Designer: John Kelly
Additional artwork: Micheal Woods and John Kelly
Research: Liz Ferguson and Simon Beecroft

Editorial Director: Ruth Binney
Production: Barry Baker and Janice Storr

Originated by CLG, Verona, Italy
Printed and bound in Italy by Officine Grafiche De Agostini—Novara

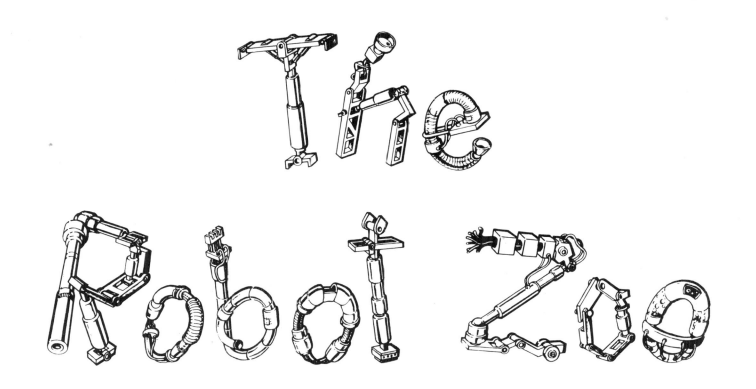

The Robot Zoo

John Kelly
Dr. Philip Whitfield and Obin

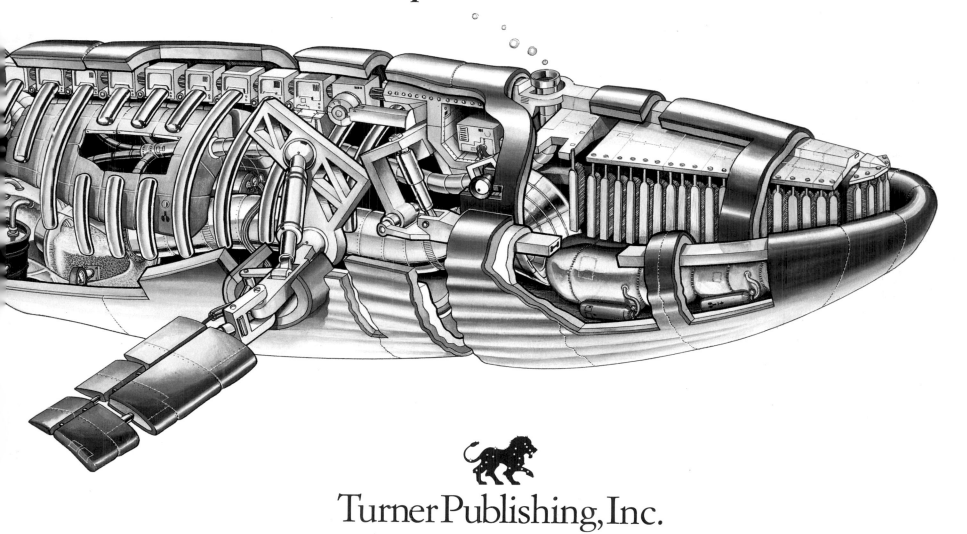

Turner Publishing, Inc.

ATLANTA

Contents

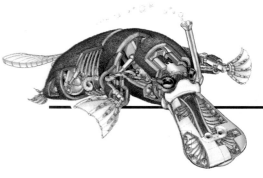

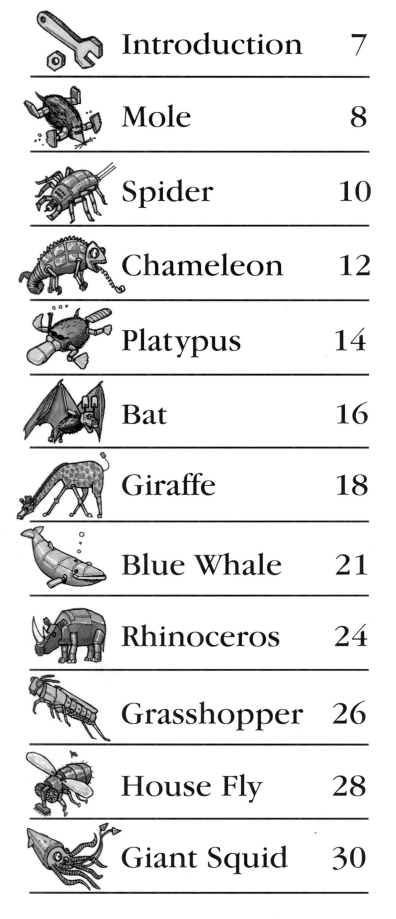

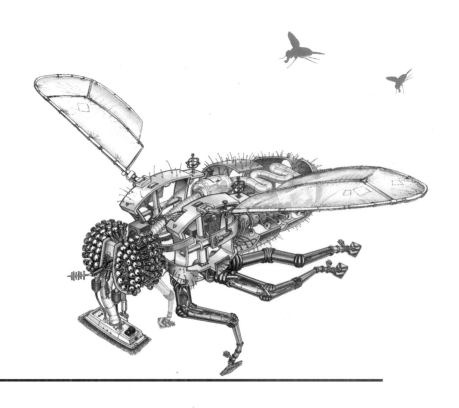

Introduction

Have you ever wondered how a gull's wings work or how a giant squid propels itself through the water, how a spider can spin a web or how a grasshopper sings? These are just some of the amazing things that the animals in this book can do. Nature is a master engineer and has designed every animal to be specially suited to its surroundings. You'd have thought that each animal was a carefully planned machine, because every one is specifically adapted to its individual lifestyle.

In *The Robot Zoo*, this is exactly what has been done. We have copied nature's own designs and have made animals into machines. Looking at them will help you to understand how real animals work, because inside they're all separated into easily recognizable parts. We've used shock absorbers for the giraffe's horns, strong armor for the rhino's thick skin, and huge digging tools for the mole's front claws. We've even included a glossary at the back to help explain all the details.

All animals move, breathe, eat, and avoid being eaten, and every creature manages to survive successfully in its own special way. Discover for yourself the fascinating ways that animals really work.

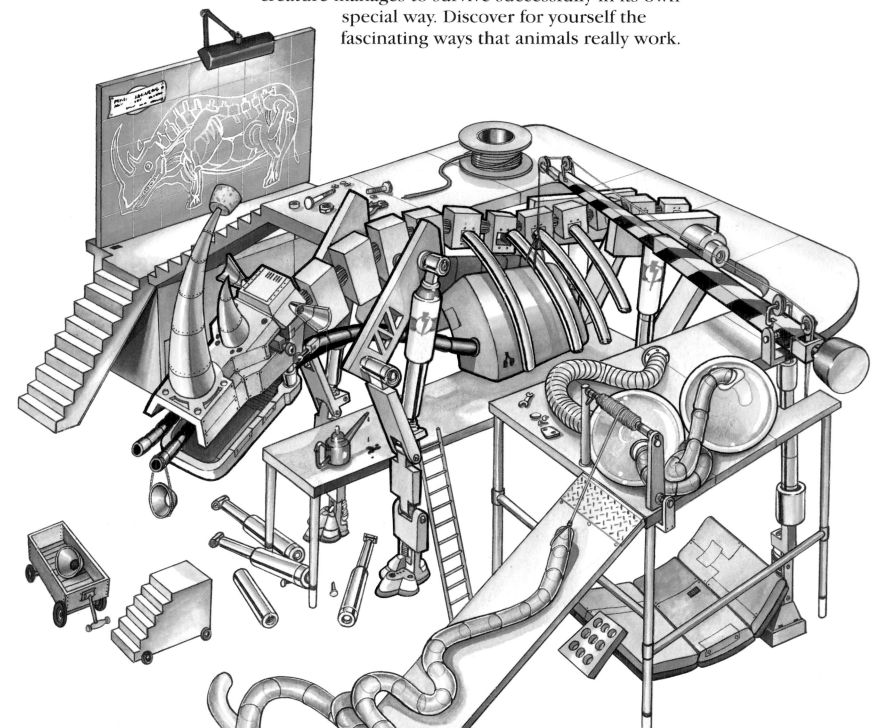

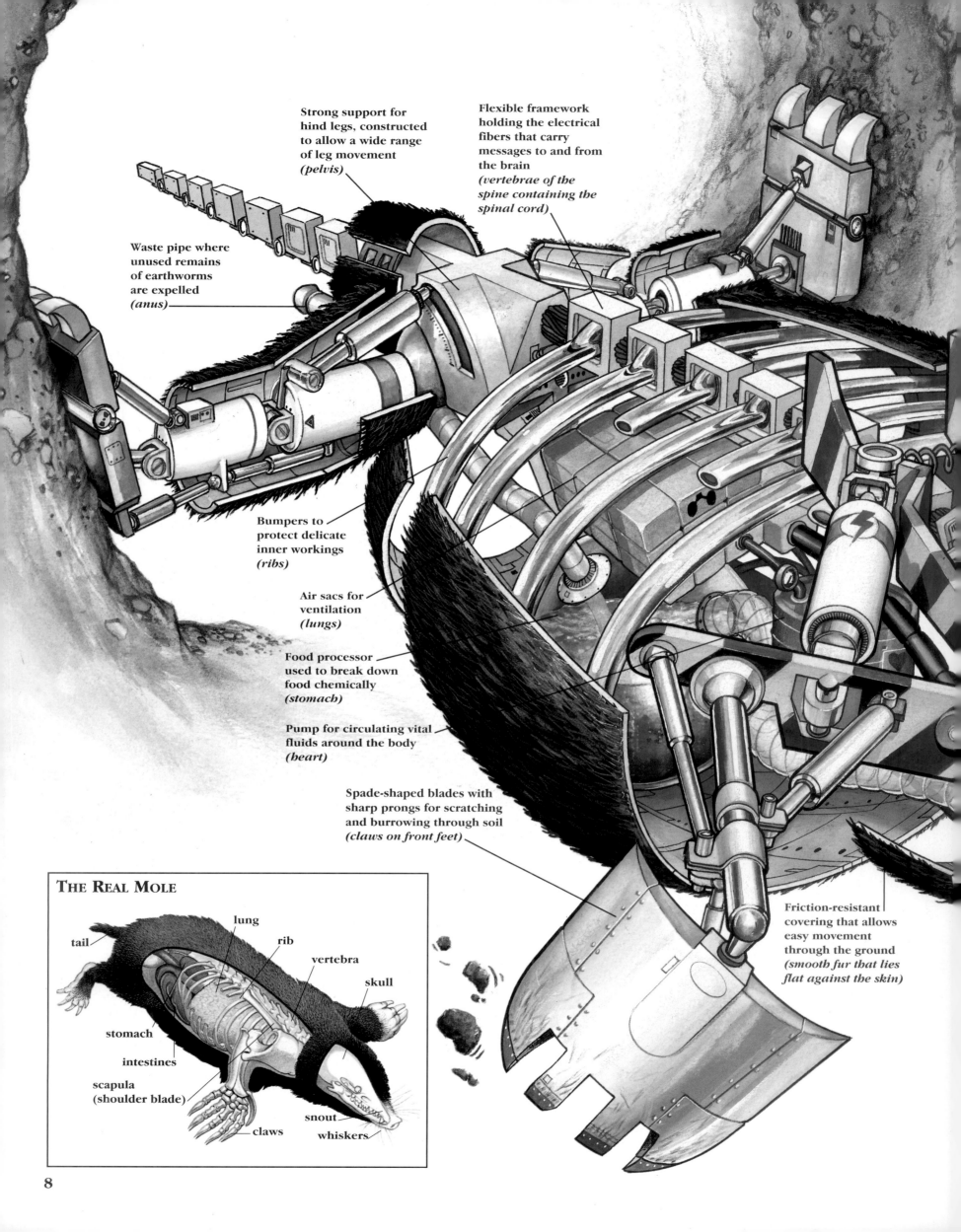

Strong support for hind legs, constructed to allow a wide range of leg movement (*pelvis*)

Flexible framework holding the electrical fibers that carry messages to and from the brain (*vertebrae of the spine containing the spinal cord*)

Waste pipe where unused remains of earthworms are expelled (*anus*)

Bumpers to protect delicate inner workings (*ribs*)

Air sacs for ventilation (*lungs*)

Food processor used to break down food chemically (*stomach*)

Pump for circulating vital fluids around the body (*heart*)

Spade-shaped blades with sharp prongs for scratching and burrowing through soil (*claws on front feet*)

Friction-resistant covering that allows easy movement through the ground (*smooth fur that lies flat against the skin*)

THE REAL MOLE

tail

lung

rib

vertebra

skull

stomach

intestines

scapula (shoulder blade)

claws

snout

whiskers

8

Mole

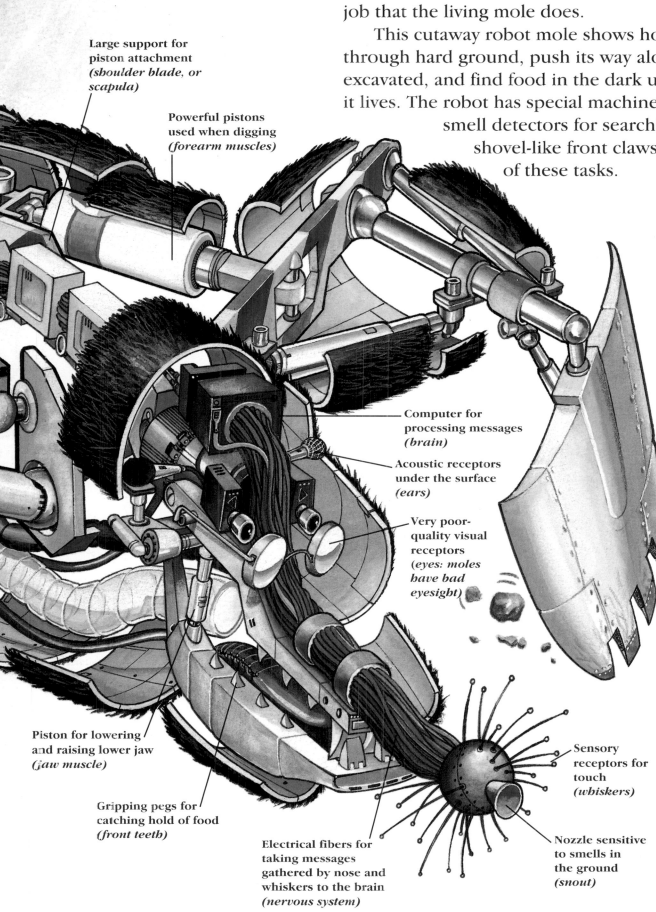

To enable the front arms to dig properly in the soil, the robot must brace itself against the sides of the tunnel. This prevents the robot from being pushed backward as the blades move forward. You can see that the hind legs are attached with swivel joints, which means they can be rotated sideways and pushed against the sides of the tunnel. The robot mole can then burrow efficiently.

A mole is a mammal that is related to insect-eating animals like shrews and hedgehogs. Moles are adapted for a life underground, burrowing in the soil. It is no surprise that the machines we use for boring railroad or mining tunnels are sometimes called mechanical moles—they do exactly the same job that the living mole does.

This cutaway robot mole shows how the animal can burrow through hard ground, push its way along the tunnel it has excavated, and find food in the dark underground world in which it lives. The robot has special machinery, like the extrasensitive smell detectors for searching out earthworms and the shovel-like front claws for digging, to carry out each of these tasks.

Large support for piston attachment (**shoulder blade, or scapula**)

Powerful pistons used when digging (**forearm muscles**)

Because the mole lives underground in the dark, vision is not very useful. Although it has no outer ear, which could be damaged during burrowing, its hearing is good. However, the mole relies mostly on its senses of smell and touch, which are especially developed in its nose and whiskers.

Computer for processing messages (**brain**)

Acoustic receptors under the surface (**ears**)

Very poor-quality visual receptors (**eyes: moles have bad eyesight**)

Piston for lowering and raising lower jaw (**jaw muscle**)

Gripping pegs for catching hold of food (**front teeth**)

Electrical fibers for taking messages gathered by nose and whiskers to the brain (**nervous system**)

Sensory receptors for touch (**whiskers**)

Nozzle sensitive to smells in the ground (**snout**)

MOLE FACTS
Country: worldwide
Habitat: temperate climates, underground
Length: up to 9 in. (23 cm)
Weight: up to 3 oz. (85 g)
Closest relative: shrew

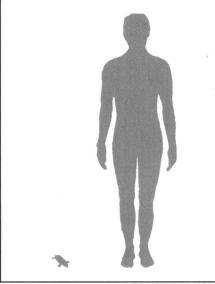

Spider

Even though some spiders are less than one-sixteenth of an inch across, you can see from this robot spider that they are highly complicated machines. Spiders are often mistakenly thought of as insects. In fact, they are arachnids, a completely different group of joint-limbed arthropods that have eight legs. There are over thirty thousand different kinds of spiders. Some of the larger spiders can live for twenty-five years.

All spiders are predators. This means they have to find their food, trap it, and kill it. Spiders eat insects, which are not the easiest animals to hunt—as you would know if you've ever tried to catch a fly. So almost all spiders produce silk threads that they form into a web. This helps them catch insects that fly past. But have you ever wondered how the spider makes its silk threads? And why insects get caught in them? Or how the spider kills its prey?

This robot version of a typical spider shows the types of machinery a spider needs to build webs, feed, and make baby spiders.

How do spiders know how to make a web, what food they can eat, and where to catch it? Their brains are like preprogrammed computers. They know instinctively how to behave. In a given situation, the spider's brain tells it what to do.

Sensory receptors used to locate vibrations of either prey or danger *(sensitive hairs)*

Preprogrammed mini-computer *(brain)*

Syringes to inject poison *(chelicerae; fangs)*

Suction nozzle for intake of food that has been dissolved *(mouth)*

Jointed probes with sensors *(pedipalps that hold prey down and that can sense surroundings)*

Eight visual receptors on turrets, pointing in different directions *(eyes)*

Hollow tubes that can be moved by hydraulics *(legs moved with muscles)*

Spiders inject their prey with poison to kill it, and with substances called digestive enzymes that break down the insect's insides into a kind of soup. Once this has happened, the spider sucks up the liquid that has been made.

10

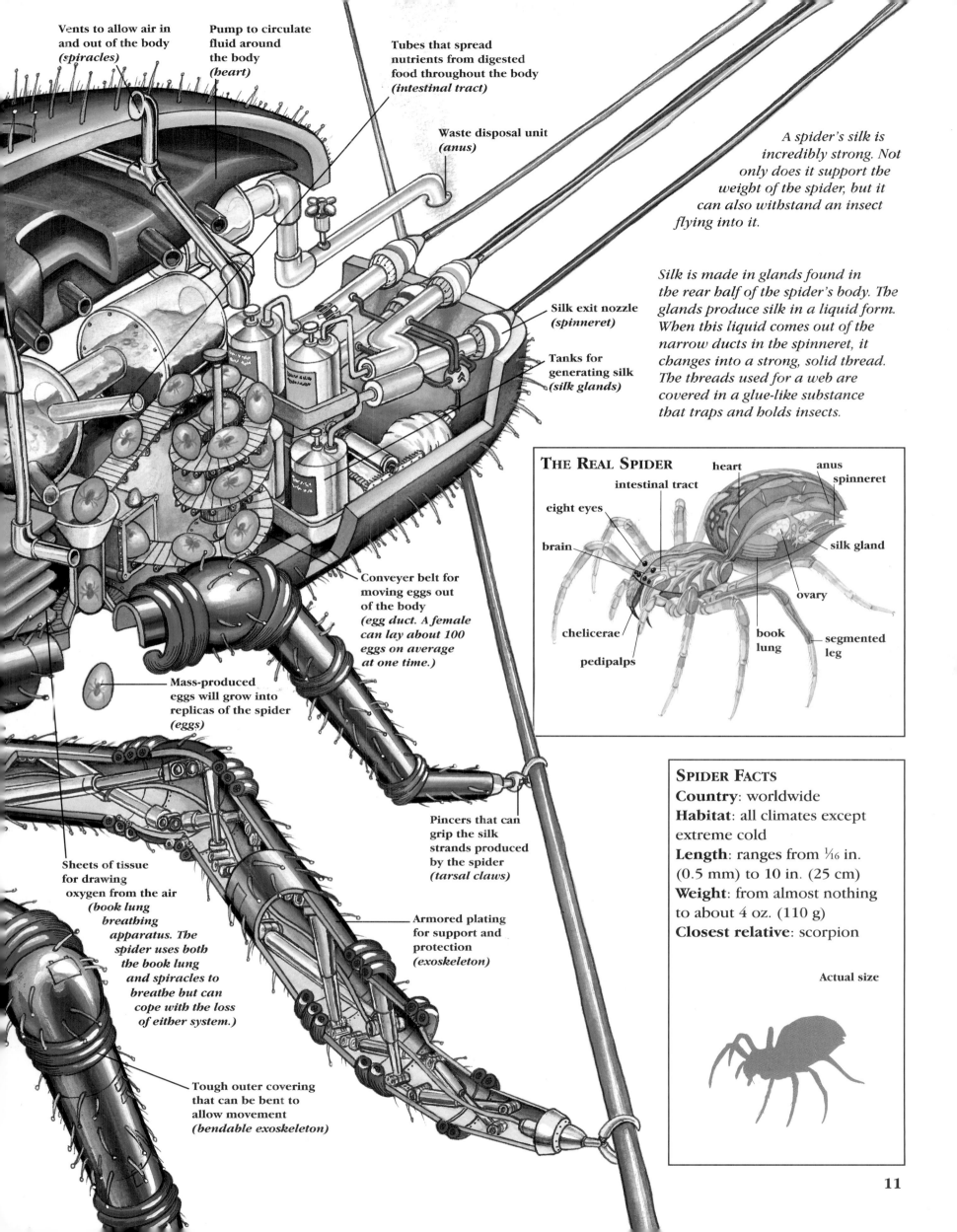

Vents to allow air in and out of the body (spiracles)

Pump to circulate fluid around the body (heart)

Tubes that spread nutrients from digested food throughout the body (intestinal tract)

Waste disposal unit (anus)

Silk exit nozzle (spinneret)

Tanks for generating silk (silk glands)

Conveyer belt for moving eggs out of the body (egg duct. A female can lay about 100 eggs on average at one time.)

Mass-produced eggs will grow into replicas of the spider (eggs)

Pincers that can grip the silk strands produced by the spider (tarsal claws)

Sheets of tissue for drawing oxygen from the air (book lung breathing apparatus. The spider uses both the book lung and spiracles to breathe but can cope with the loss of either system.)

Armored plating for support and protection (exoskeleton)

Tough outer covering that can be bent to allow movement (bendable exoskeleton)

A spider's silk is incredibly strong. Not only does it support the weight of the spider, but it can also withstand an insect flying into it.

Silk is made in glands found in the rear half of the spider's body. The glands produce silk in a liquid form. When this liquid comes out of the narrow ducts in the spinneret, it changes into a strong, solid thread. The threads used for a web are covered in a glue-like substance that traps and holds insects.

THE REAL SPIDER

heart · anus · spinneret · intestinal tract · eight eyes · brain · chelicerae · pedipalps · silk gland · ovary · book lung · segmented leg

SPIDER FACTS
Country: worldwide
Habitat: all climates except extreme cold
Length: ranges from 1/16 in. (0.5 mm) to 10 in. (25 cm)
Weight: from almost nothing to about 4 oz. (110 g)
Closest relative: scorpion

Actual size

11

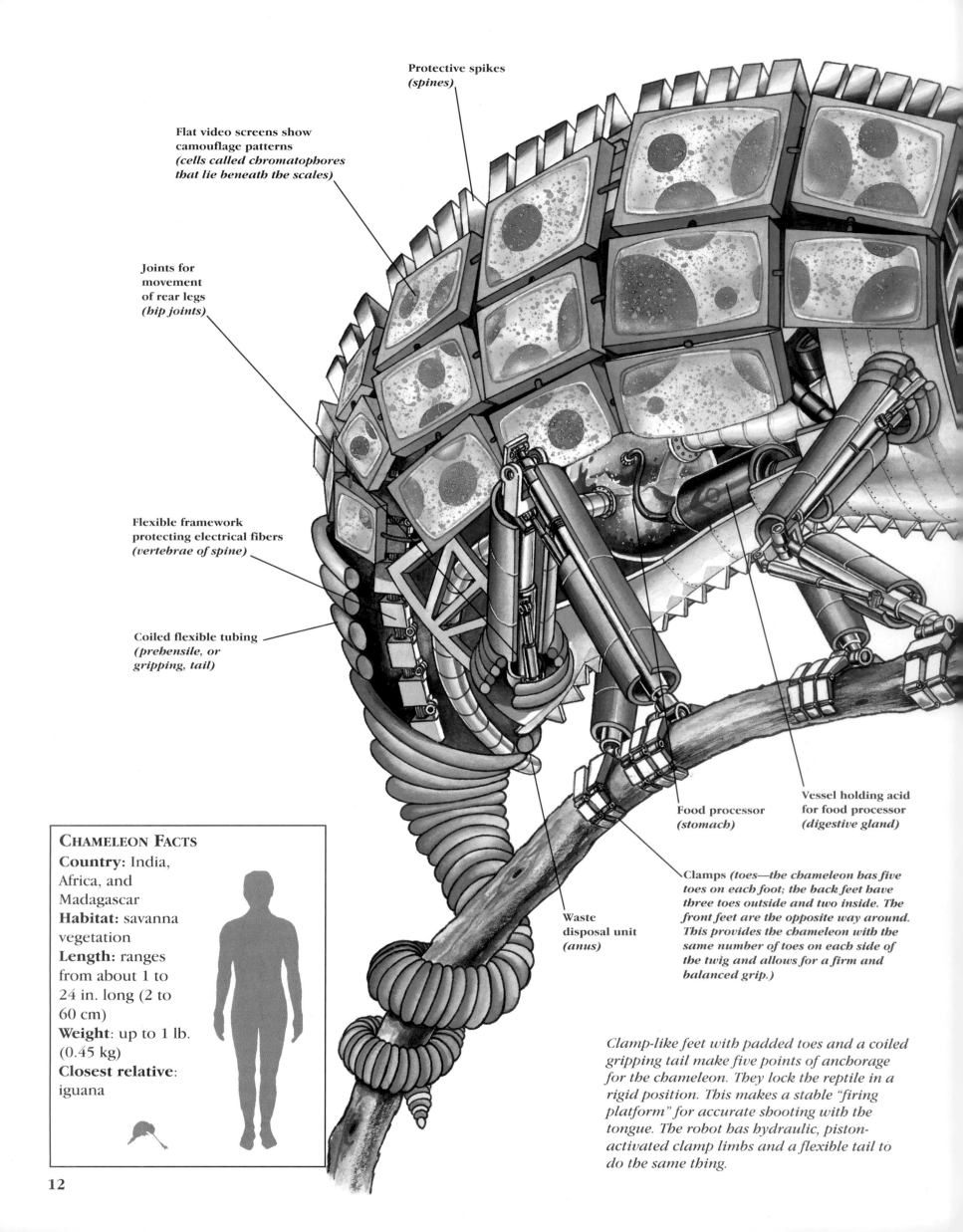

Protective spikes
(spines)

Flat video screens show
camouflage patterns
*(cells called chromatophores
that lie beneath the scales)*

Joints for
movement
of rear legs
(hip joints)

Flexible framework
protecting electrical fibers
(vertebrae of spine)

Coiled flexible tubing
*(prehensile, or
gripping, tail)*

CHAMELEON FACTS
Country: India,
Africa, and
Madagascar
Habitat: savanna
vegetation
Length: ranges
from about 1 to
24 in. long (2 to
60 cm)
Weight: up to 1 lb.
(0.45 kg)
Closest relative:
iguana

Food processor
(stomach)

Vessel holding acid
for food processor
(digestive gland)

Clamps *(toes—the chameleon has five
toes on each foot; the back feet have
three toes outside and two inside. The
front feet are the opposite way around.
This provides the chameleon with the
same number of toes on each side of
the twig and allows for a firm and
balanced grip.)*

Waste
disposal unit
(anus)

*Clamp-like feet with padded toes and a coiled
gripping tail make five points of anchorage
for the chameleon. They lock the reptile in a
rigid position. This makes a stable "firing
platform" for accurate shooting with the
tongue. The robot has hydraulic, piston-
activated clamp limbs and a flexible tail to
do the same thing.*

Chameleon

Mini-computer
(brain)

**Electrical
control fibers
(nerve bundle)**

**Universal joints for
visual receptors
(eye muscles that
allow the eyes to
move in all
directions)**

**Protective
sleeves for visual
receptors
(eyelids)**

**Visual
receptors
(eyes)**

**Air and
scent inlets
(nostrils)**

**Spike around
which the spring
coil is wound
(bone)**

**Coil
(extendable tongue)**

**Spring-loaded
mechanism
(muscles forcing
out the tongue)**

**Air intake pipe
(trachea)**

**Food intake pipe
(esophagus)**

**Flypaper
(sticky tongue end)**

A **chameleon is a reptile with two noteworthy skills.** First, it can change its skin color and pattern to match its surroundings—mottled brown on a tree trunk, or bright green on a leafy twig. Second, it catches insects in a unique way. After walking very slowly toward an insect that it has located using its large, separately movable eyes, the chameleon shoots out an immensely long, sticky-tipped tongue to trap its prey. Based on the design of a real rainforest chameleon, this robot can perform both of the reptile's party tricks.

Although the chameleon is the same as other reptiles in that it is cold-blooded and it lays eggs, it is also part of a special group of reptiles called lizards. Lizards feed at night and are very good climbers. Because of its ability to change color, the chameleon is one of the most talented lizards.

The robot's two pivoting visual sensors pick up an excellent picture of the world around it. Control fibers from the sensors link back to the mini-computer. This, via other fibers, controls the images on banks of tiny video screens that cover the robot's surface. With multiscreen picture software, the computer makes the surface look like the surroundings. In the real animal, the eyes, brain, and the nerves that run to color cells in the skin do the same thing.

THE REAL CHAMELEON

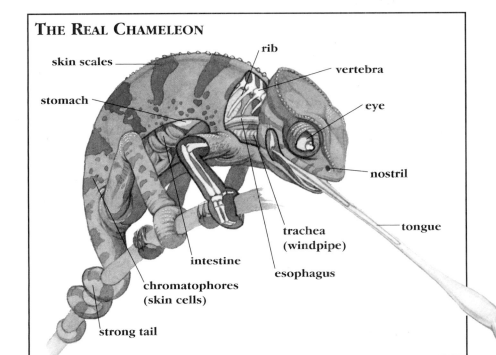

skin scales

rib

vertebra

stomach

eye

nostril

**trachea
(windpipe)**

tongue

intestine

esophagus

**chromatophores
(skin cells)**

strong tail

The chameleon's tongue is built out of a muscular tube wrapped around a long, thin, tapering bone that lies in the floor of the animal's mouth. When the tongue muscles are triggered to fire, they squeeze tightly on the bone. This makes the whole tongue shoot out like an orange seed squeezed between your fingers. In the robot, a spring-loaded mechanism triggers the food-capturing machinery, which is a long spring that uncoils and shoots forward. Good aim is achieved because the spring is coiled around a forward-pointing spike. The spring has a sticky end that allows the chameleon to capture a robot fly.

13

Platypus

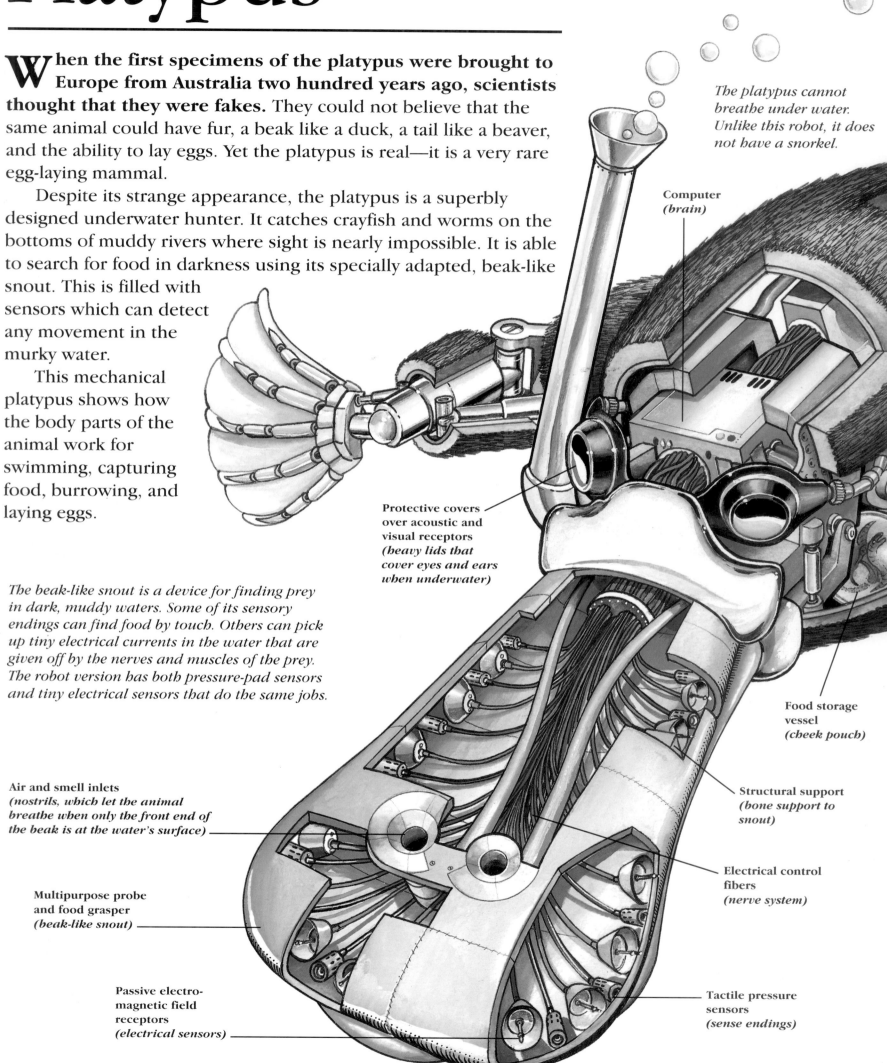

When the first specimens of the platypus were brought to Europe from Australia two hundred years ago, scientists thought that they were fakes. They could not believe that the same animal could have fur, a beak like a duck, a tail like a beaver, and the ability to lay eggs. Yet the platypus is real—it is a very rare egg-laying mammal.

Despite its strange appearance, the platypus is a superbly designed underwater hunter. It catches crayfish and worms on the bottoms of muddy rivers where sight is nearly impossible. It is able to search for food in darkness using its specially adapted, beak-like snout. This is filled with sensors which can detect any movement in the murky water.

This mechanical platypus shows how the body parts of the animal work for swimming, capturing food, burrowing, and laying eggs.

The beak-like snout is a device for finding prey in dark, muddy waters. Some of its sensory endings can find food by touch. Others can pick up tiny electrical currents in the water that are given off by the nerves and muscles of the prey. The robot version has both pressure-pad sensors and tiny electrical sensors that do the same jobs.

The platypus cannot breathe under water. Unlike this robot, it does not have a snorkel.

Computer (brain)

Protective covers over acoustic and visual receptors *(heavy lids that cover eyes and ears when underwater)*

Food storage vessel *(cheek pouch)*

Structural support *(bone support to snout)*

Electrical control fibers *(nerve system)*

Tactile pressure sensors *(sense endings)*

Air and smell inlets *(nostrils, which let the animal breathe when only the front end of the beak is at the water's surface)*

Multipurpose probe and food grasper *(beak-like snout)*

Passive electro-magnetic field receptors *(electrical sensors)*

14

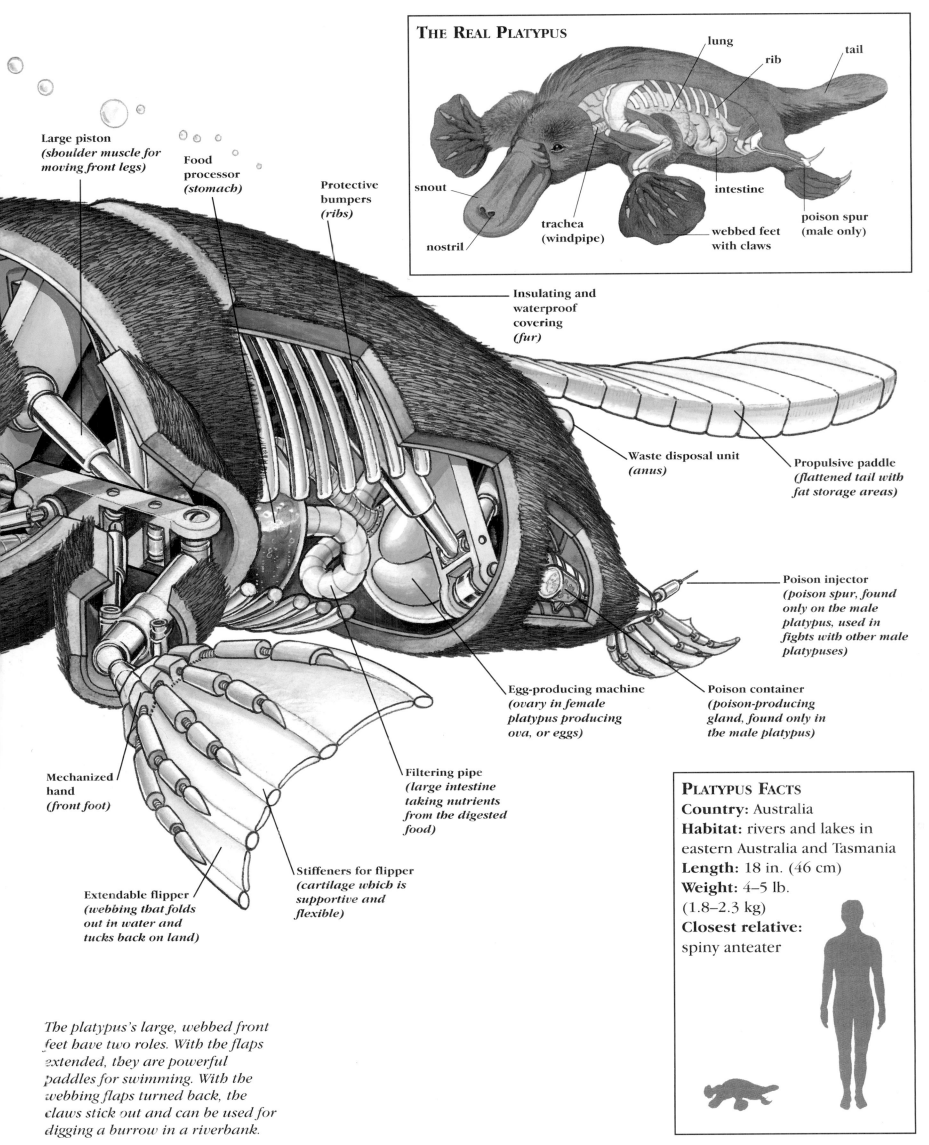

Large piston
(shoulder muscle for moving front legs)

Food processor
(stomach)

Protective bumpers
(ribs)

THE REAL PLATYPUS

lung

rib

tail

snout

trachea
(windpipe)

nostril

intestine

webbed feet
with claws

poison spur
(male only)

Insulating and waterproof covering
(fur)

Waste disposal unit
(anus)

Propulsive paddle
(flattened tail with fat storage areas)

Poison injector
(poison spur, found only on the male platypus, used in fights with other male platypuses)

Egg-producing machine
(ovary in female platypus producing ova, or eggs)

Poison container
(poison-producing gland, found only in the male platypus)

Mechanized hand
(front foot)

Filtering pipe
(large intestine taking nutrients from the digested food)

Extendable flipper
(webbing that folds out in water and tucks back on land)

Stiffeners for flipper
(cartilage which is supportive and flexible)

PLATYPUS FACTS
Country: Australia
Habitat: rivers and lakes in eastern Australia and Tasmania
Length: 18 in. (46 cm)
Weight: 4–5 lb. (1.8–2.3 kg)
Closest relative: spiny anteater

The platypus's large, webbed front feet have two roles. With the flaps extended, they are powerful paddles for swimming. With the webbing flaps turned back, the claws stick out and can be used for digging a burrow in a riverbank.

15

Bat

While birds rule the daytime skies, the bat, a flying mammal, is master of the air at night. Its leathery wings are made of flexible skin flaps that stretch between the incredibly long fingers of the bat's hands, making them very strong and efficient for flying. During the day, bats usually roost in large groups in caves, attics, or hollow trees, hanging upside-down with their clawed hind feet.

Most bats hunt for food such as moths, but some have different ways of feeding. Vampire bats from South and Central America feed on the blood of people, cows, and horses. Fruit bats, sometimes called flying foxes, feed on the fruit of tropical trees. Hunting bats catch mice on the ground or fish that swim near the surface of a lake.

Bats find their food in complete darkness using a system called echolocation. The bat sends out very high-pitched noises (ultrasonic sounds) that "echo" or bounce off its prey. Using the echoes to locate its prey, the bat then chases, captures, and eats it.

The "fingers" that make up the robot's wings are lightweight tubes. The material between the tubes acts like a sail on a hang-glider, stretching back onto the hind legs and between the hind legs and tail. Pistons attached to the robot's body move the tubes of the wings up and down in flight.

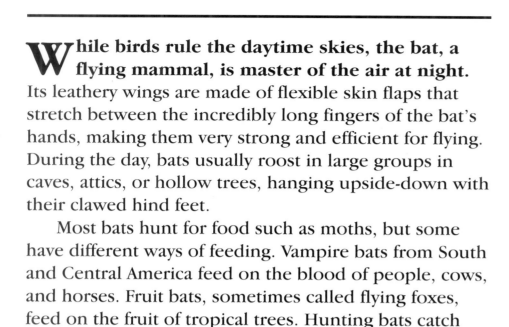

Strut
(second finger)

Strut
(third finger)

Strut
(fifth finger)

Strut
(fourth finger)

Strong, flexible material stretched over struts
(wing membrane)

Long support strut
(tail)

Filtering pipe
(intestines taking nutrients from the digested food)

Extra strut for added membrane support
(calcar)

Forward-facing clamps for gripping branches
(claws)

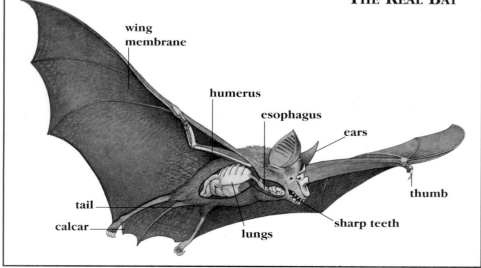

THE REAL BAT

wing membrane

humerus

esophagus

ears

thumb

tail

calcar

lungs

sharp teeth

16

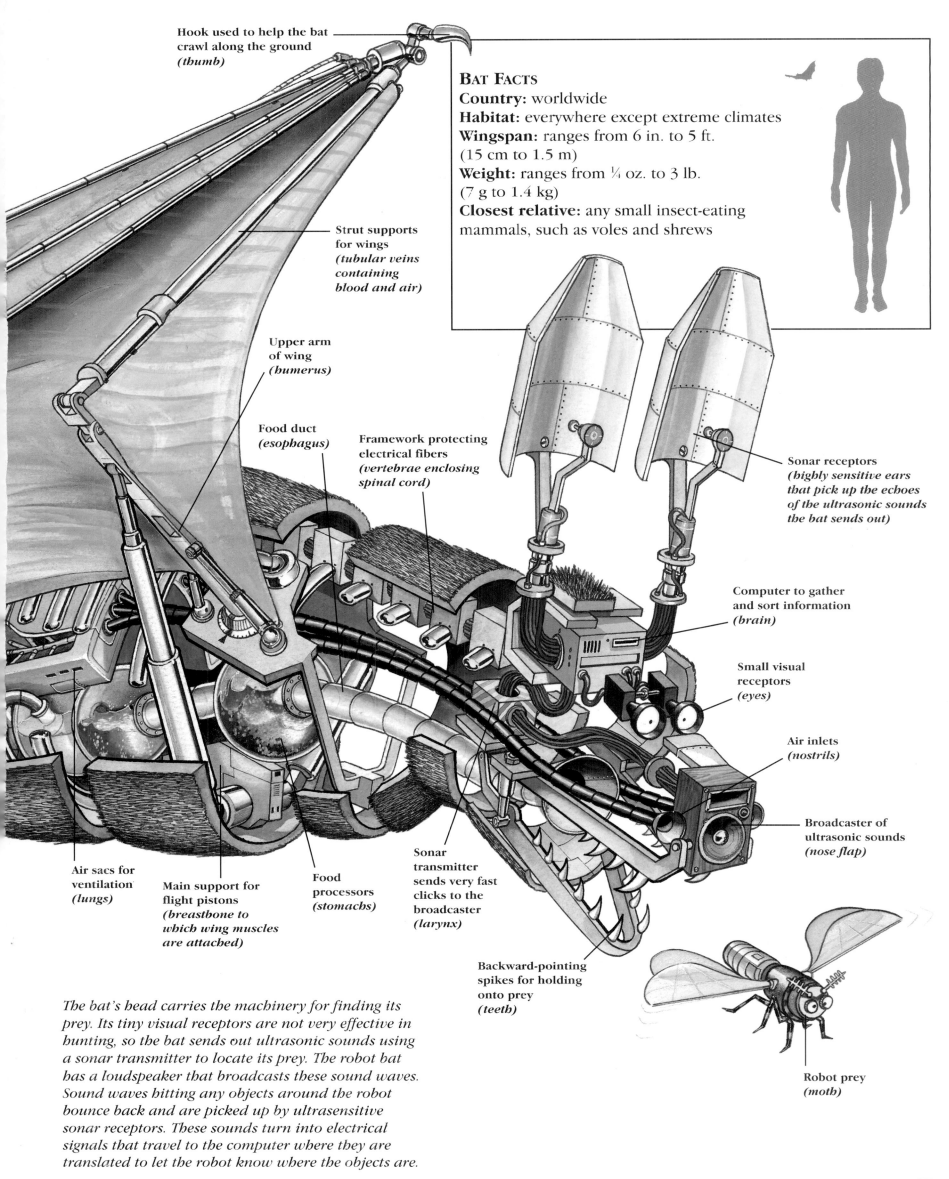

Hook used to help the bat crawl along the ground
(thumb)

BAT FACTS
Country: worldwide
Habitat: everywhere except extreme climates
Wingspan: ranges from 6 in. to 5 ft.
(15 cm to 1.5 m)
Weight: ranges from ¼ oz. to 3 lb.
(7 g to 1.4 kg)
Closest relative: any small insect-eating
mammals, such as voles and shrews

Strut supports
for wings
*(tubular veins
containing
blood and air)*

Upper arm
of wing
(humerus)

Food duct
(esophagus)

Framework protecting
electrical fibers
*(vertebrae enclosing
spinal cord)*

Sonar receptors
*(highly sensitive ears
that pick up the echoes
of the ultrasonic sounds
the bat sends out)*

Computer to gather
and sort information
(brain)

Small visual
receptors
(eyes)

Air inlets
(nostrils)

Broadcaster of
ultrasonic sounds
(nose flap)

Air sacs for
ventilation
(lungs)

Main support for
flight pistons
*(breastbone to
which wing muscles
are attached)*

Food
processors
(stomachs)

Sonar
transmitter
sends very fast
clicks to the
broadcaster
(larynx)

Backward-pointing
spikes for holding
onto prey
(teeth)

Robot prey
(moth)

*The bat's head carries the machinery for finding its
prey. Its tiny visual receptors are not very effective in
hunting, so the bat sends out ultrasonic sounds using
a sonar transmitter to locate its prey. The robot bat
has a loudspeaker that broadcasts these sound waves.
Sound waves hitting any objects around the robot
bounce back and are picked up by ultrasensitive
sonar receptors. These sounds turn into electrical
signals that travel to the computer where they are
translated to let the robot know where the objects are.*

Giraffe

Giraffes are the tallest animals on earth. This is an advantage in the wild, but it can create a lot of problems, too. To cope with the difficulties caused by their amazing height, giraffes have special solutions. This robot giraffe shows just how unusual the natural systems of this animal have to be for it to be able to move and work successfully.

First of all, the giraffe has an incredibly strong heart to pump blood up its long neck and to its brain. When the giraffe bends down, the surge of blood to its head could cause problems with pressure, so the arteries at the base of the neck slow the flow of the blood until the animal brings its neck up again. Look at the robot giraffe's neck to see the many pressure valves that regulate the blood as it is pumped up the long neck tube.

You might wonder why the giraffe doesn't fall over, since the front part of its body is so much bigger than the back. In fact, most of the giraffe's weight is at the back. The weight of the neck and head is carried over its long front legs and is supported by powerful muscles that are attached to its shoulders and backbone. This allows the giraffe to stand tall and eat leaves that are far beyond the reach of other animals.

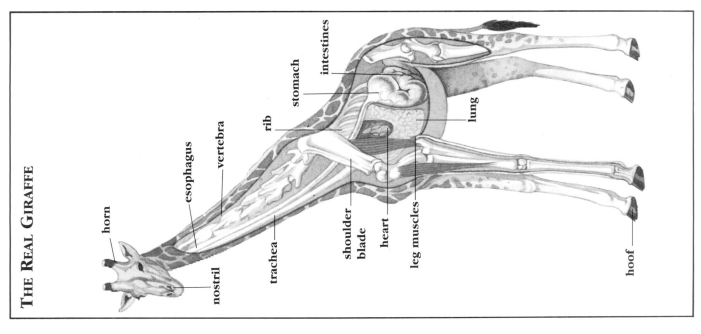

THE REAL GIRAFFE

horn

nostril

esophagus

vertebra

trachea

shoulder blade

heart

leg muscles

rib

stomach

intestines

lung

hoof

Movable acoustic receptors for following sounds (*ears*)

Buffers (*horns*)

Visual receptors (*eyes*)

Long, flexible pad for grabbing food and water (*tongue*)

Files for grinding up tough plants (*back teeth*)

Air inlets (*nostrils*)

Sharp blades for snipping leaves (*front teeth*)

Air intake pipe (*trachea*)

Food is squeezed down through a flexible tube (*esophagus*)

High-pressure flexible tubing (*artery*)

Flexible framework fits together to support the neck (*neck vertebrae*)

Valves stop the fluid from falling back down the neck between the beats of the pump (*valves in arteries*)

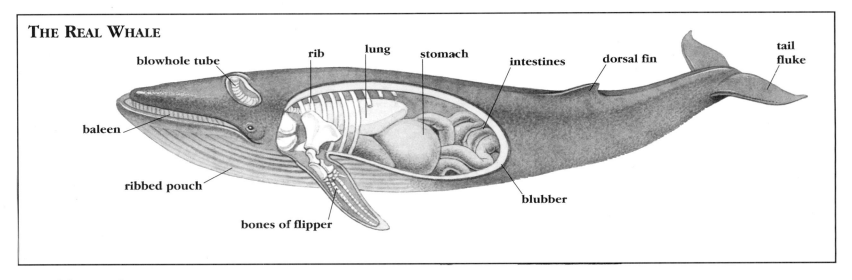

THE REAL WHALE

blowhole tube

rib   lung   stomach   intestines   dorsal fin   tail fluke

baleen

ribbed pouch

bones of flipper

blubber

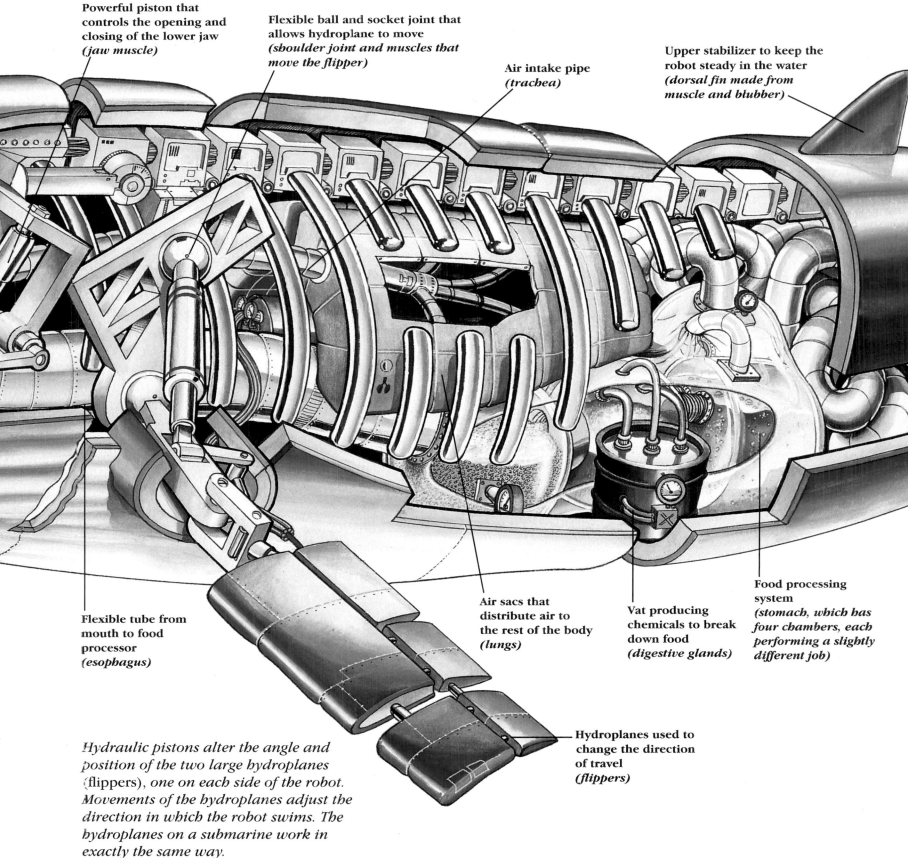

Powerful piston that controls the opening and closing of the lower jaw *(jaw muscle)*

Flexible ball and socket joint that allows hydroplane to move *(shoulder joint and muscles that move the flipper)*

Air intake pipe *(trachea)*

Upper stabilizer to keep the robot steady in the water *(dorsal fin made from muscle and blubber)*

Flexible tube from mouth to food processor *(esophagus)*

Air sacs that distribute air to the rest of the body *(lungs)*

Vat producing chemicals to break down food *(digestive glands)*

Food processing system *(stomach, which has four chambers, each performing a slightly different job)*

Hydroplanes used to change the direction of travel *(flippers)*

Hydraulic pistons alter the angle and position of the two large hydroplanes (flippers), one on each side of the robot. Movements of the hydroplanes adjust the direction in which the robot swims. The hydroplanes on a submarine work in exactly the same way.

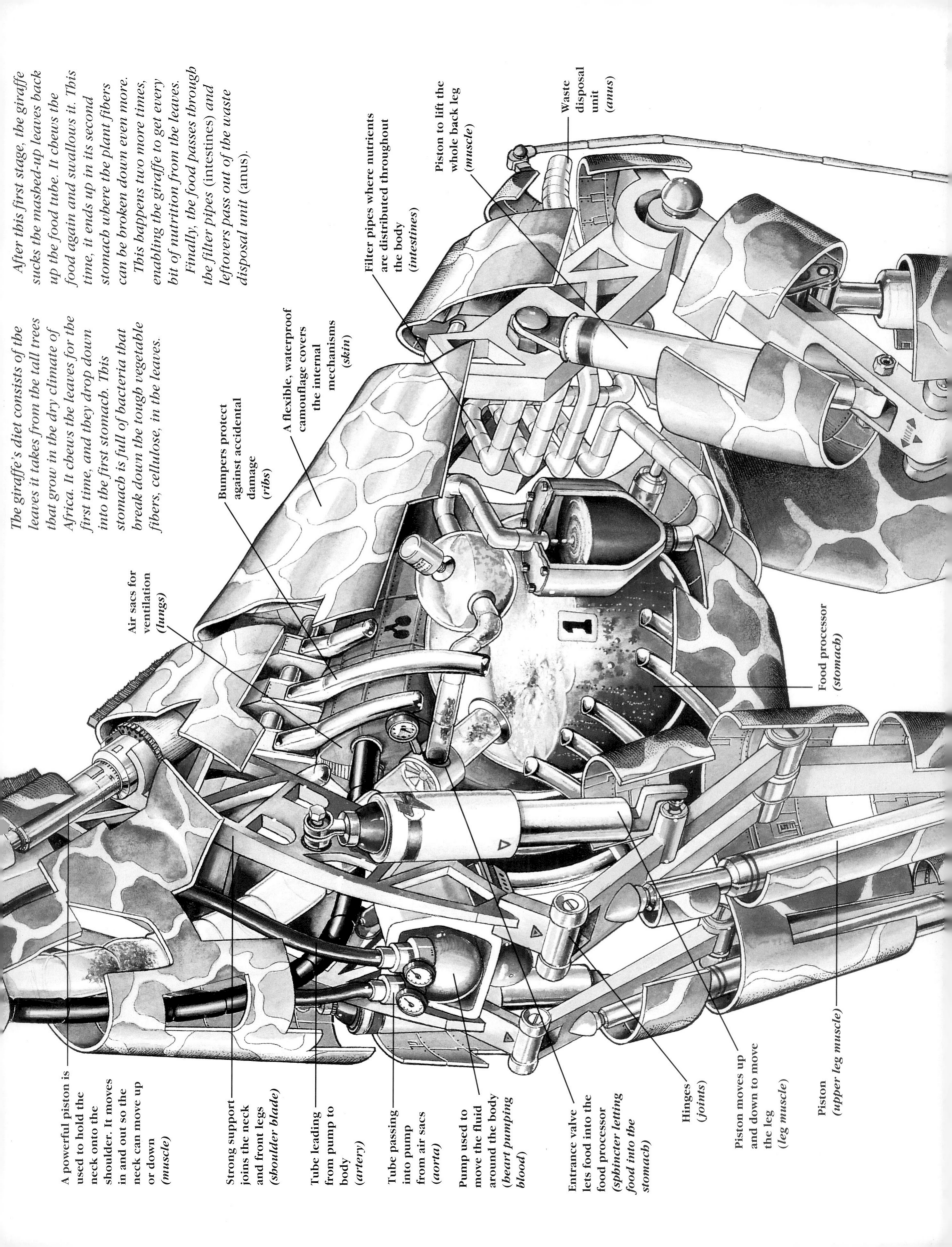

The giraffe's diet consists of the leaves it takes from the tall trees that grow in the dry climate of Africa. It chews the leaves for the first time, and they drop down into the first stomach. This stomach is full of bacteria that break down the tough vegetable fibers, cellulose, in the leaves.

After this first stage, the giraffe sucks the mashed-up leaves back up the food tube. It chews the food again and swallows it. This time, it ends up in its second stomach where the plant fibers can be broken down even more. This happens two more times, enabling the giraffe to get every bit of nutrition from the leaves. Finally, the food passes through the filter pipes (intestines) and leftovers pass out of the waste disposal unit (anus).

Filter pipes where nutrients are distributed throughout the body (intestines)

Waste disposal unit (anus)

Piston to lift the whole back leg (muscle)

Bumpers protect against accidental damage (ribs)

A flexible, waterproof camouflage covers the internal mechanisms (skin)

Air sacs for ventilation (lungs)

Food processor (stomach)

A powerful piston is used to hold the neck onto the shoulder. It moves in and out so the neck can move up or down (muscle)

Strong support joins the neck and front legs (shoulder blade)

Tube leading from pump to body (artery)

Tube passing into pump from air sacs (aorta)

Pump used to move the fluid around the body (heart pumping blood)

Entrance valve lets food into the food processor (sphincter letting food into the stomach)

Hinges (joints)

Piston moves up and down to move the leg (leg muscle)

Piston (upper leg muscle)

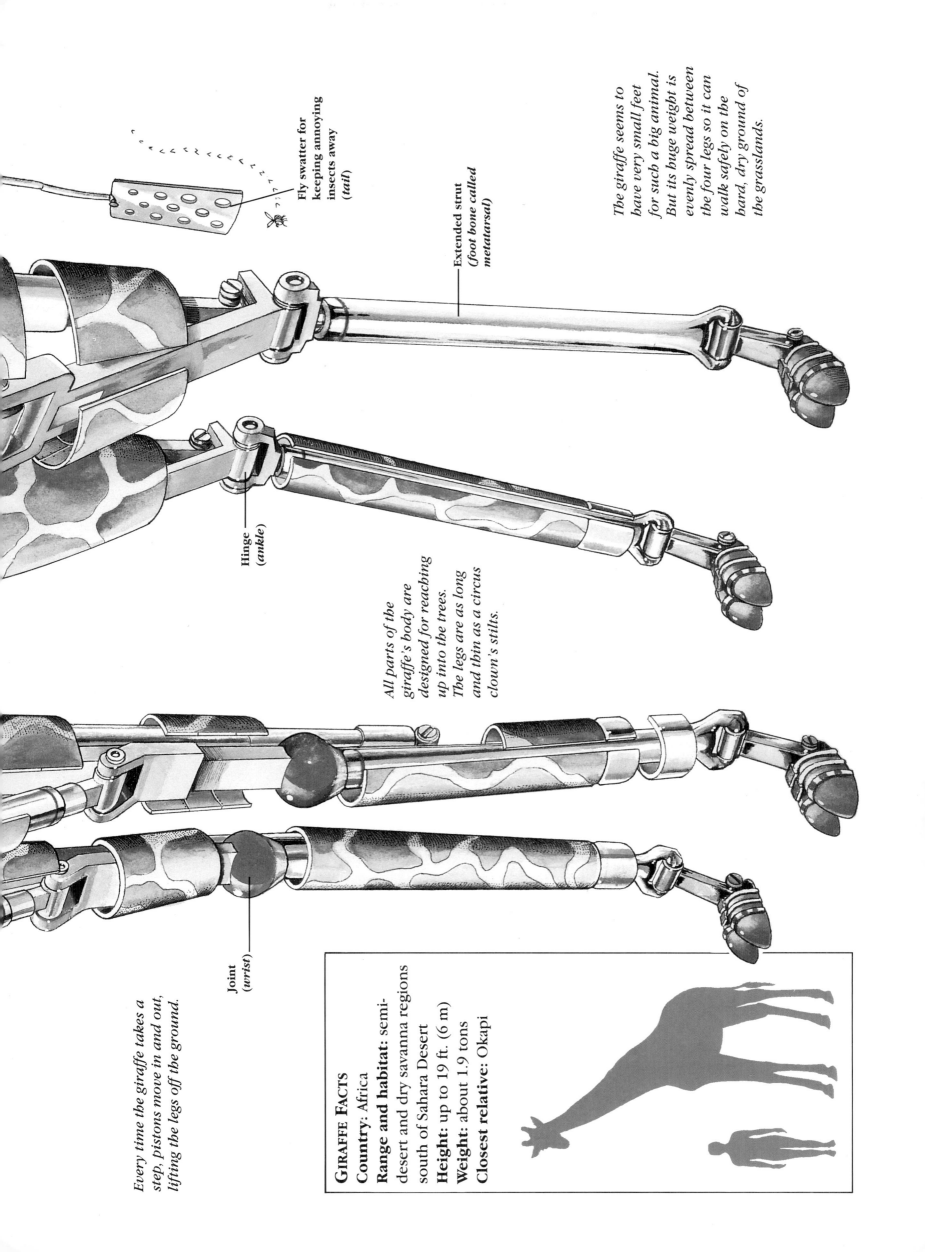

Fly swatter for keeping annoying insects away (*tail*)

Extended strut (*foot bone called metatarsal*)

The giraffe seems to have very small feet for such a big animal. But its huge weight is evenly spread between the four legs so it can walk safely on the hard, dry ground of the grasslands.

Hinge (*ankle*)

All parts of the giraffe's body are designed for reaching up into the trees. The legs are as long and thin as a circus clown's stilts.

Joint (*wrist*)

Every time the giraffe takes a step, pistons move in and out, lifting the legs off the ground.

GIRAFFE FACTS
Country: Africa
Range and habitat: semi-desert and dry savanna regions south of Sahara Desert
Height: up to 19 ft. (6 m)
Weight: about 1.9 tons
Closest relative: Okapi

Blue Whale

The largest animal that has ever lived on this planet is the extraordinary blue whale. With a body shaped like a nuclear submarine, the whale is an air-breathing mammal that spends its whole life in the sea. Taking huge breaths in through the blowhole on the top of its head, it can then dive deep into the ocean. The whale feeds underwater, gulping up countless thousands of shrimp-like animals called krill.

The blue whale is descended from land animals with four legs. Its front legs have evolved into huge flippers that control the direction of its swimming, and the hind legs have disappeared altogether. The blue whale also has a vast and powerful tail to propel it through the water.

Large computer for processing information and controlling output
(brain)

Air vent
(blowhole)

Filtering brushes
(baleen)

Expandable airbag for forcing out water from the mouth
(large tongue)

Stretchy outer covering to allow for large gulps of seawater
(skin under chin, a ribbed pouch)

Small visual receptor
(eye)

The whale feeds by swimming through krill-rich seas. It opens its huge mouth, which fills with water and krill. Closing its mouth, it traps the krill inside filters called baleen (the curtain of brushes in the robot whale). The whale then uses its powerful tongue to force the water out through the baleen. When this happens, the krill are passed down to the esophagus and swallowed.

The air vent (blowhole) at the top of the head section is connected to the air storage sacs (lungs) that provide the robot with air while it is underwater. When the whale is submerged, the vent is covered to stop water from rushing into the air supply.

The outer casing of the robot is silky smooth and slips through the water with little resistance. Underneath this thin but strong and flexible casing is a thick layer of fatty insulating material (blubber). This prevents the inner working parts of the robot from cooling down too much in the cold ocean water.

The whale's tail is made from cartilage, not from bone. Cartilage is very strong and flexible, which makes it ideal material for a propeller. The tail can measure up to 15 feet (5 meters) across and can push the whale through the water at speeds up to 20 mph (30 km/h).

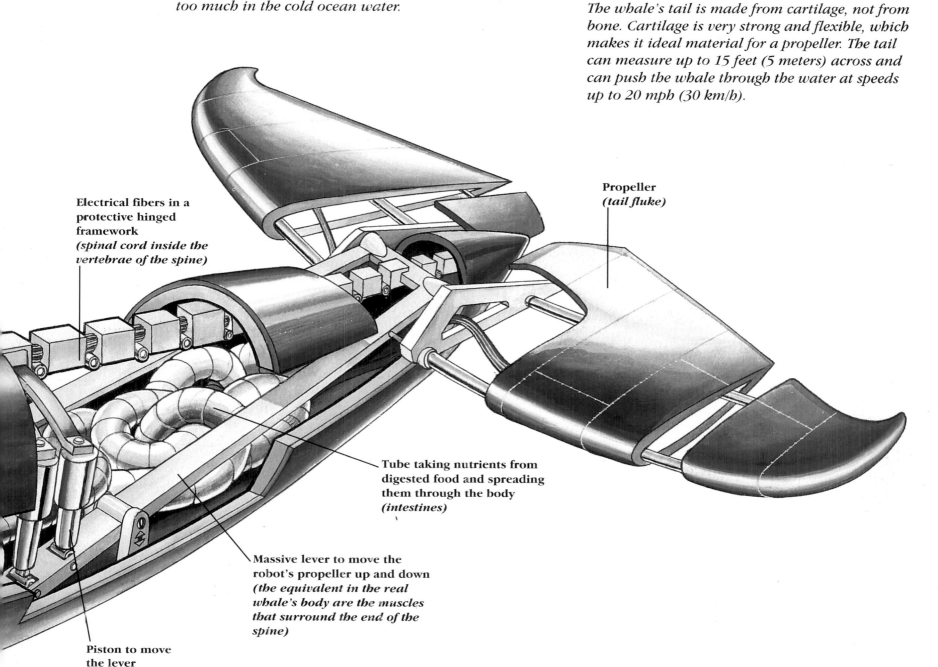

Propeller
(tail fluke)

Electrical fibers in a protective hinged framework
(spinal cord inside the vertebrae of the spine)

Tube taking nutrients from digested food and spreading them through the body
(intestines)

Massive lever to move the robot's propeller up and down
(the equivalent in the real whale's body are the muscles that surround the end of the spine)

Piston to move the lever
(muscle)

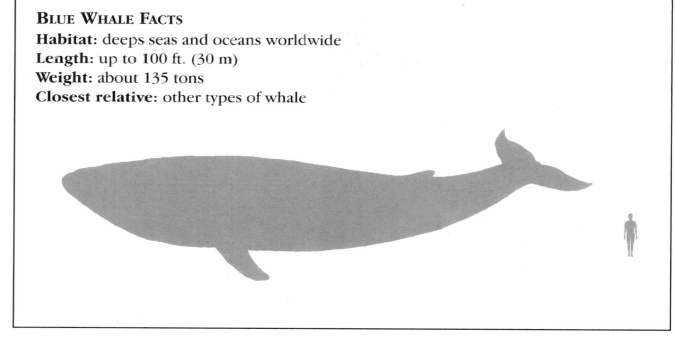

BLUE WHALE FACTS
Habitat: deeps seas and oceans worldwide
Length: up to 100 ft. (30 m)
Weight: about 135 tons
Closest relative: other types of whale

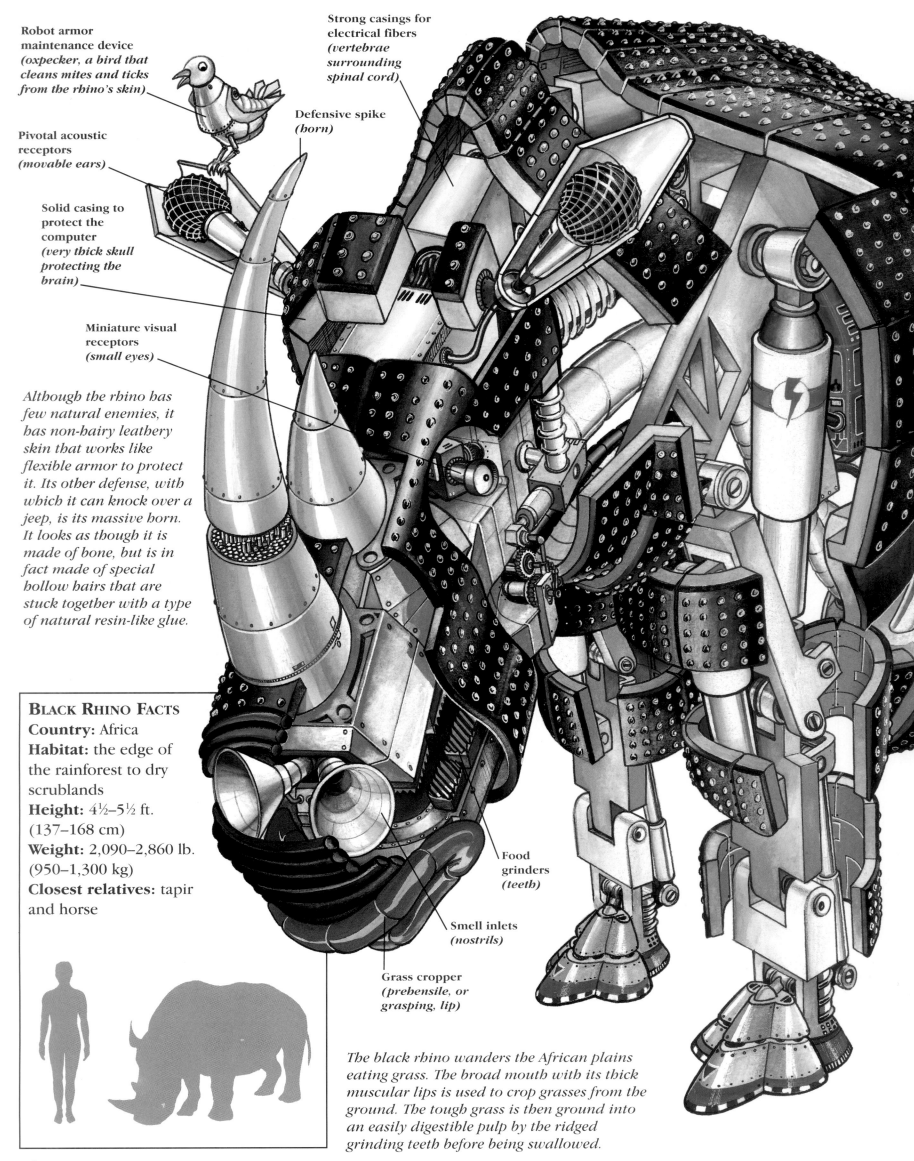

Robot armor maintenance device *(oxpecker, a bird that cleans mites and ticks from the rhino's skin)*

Strong casings for electrical fibers *(vertebrae surrounding spinal cord)*

Pivotal acoustic receptors *(movable ears)*

Defensive spike *(horn)*

Solid casing to protect the computer *(very thick skull protecting the brain)*

Miniature visual receptors *(small eyes)*

Although the rhino has few natural enemies, it has non-hairy leathery skin that works like flexible armor to protect it. Its other defense, with which it can knock over a jeep, is its massive horn. It looks as though it is made of bone, but is in fact made of special hollow hairs that are stuck together with a type of natural resin-like glue.

BLACK RHINO FACTS
Country: Africa
Habitat: the edge of the rainforest to dry scrublands
Height: 4½–5½ ft. (137–168 cm)
Weight: 2,090–2,860 lb. (950–1,300 kg)
Closest relatives: tapir and horse

Food grinders *(teeth)*

Smell inlets *(nostrils)*

Grass cropper *(prehensile, or grasping, lip)*

The black rhino wanders the African plains eating grass. The broad mouth with its thick muscular lips is used to crop grasses from the ground. The tough grass is then ground into an easily digestible pulp by the ridged grinding teeth before being swallowed.

Rhinoceros

Dual food processors
(stomachs; the rhino is a ruminant like the giraffe)

Filtering pipe
(intestines)

After the elephant, the black rhino is one of the largest land mammals on Earth. It lives in and feeds on the grassland savannas of Africa. The rhino belongs to a group of hooved animals called ungulates. Its closest relatives are tapirs and horses, but only the rhino has ended up with a very heavy body carried on immensely strong legs.

The robot rhino is massive like the living animal. Its leg supports are incredibly sturdy, and each one has three weight-bearing props at the end. Instead of leathery skin, it has studded armor for extra protection. And it has a horn, which is made of incredibly strong sections that match the strength of the hollow, hair-like fibers in the real rhino's horn. The robot rhino even has a robot tick bird called an oxpecker to clean its armor.

Ball and socket joint
(hip joint anchored into rigid pelvis)

Flies and ticks that irritate the rhino can be brushed off with the hair-tipped tail or the large hair-fringed ears. Those out of reach of either of these fly swatters are often removed by helpful tick birds such as oxpeckers. These companions perch on the rhino and eat the insects and ticks. This cleans the rhino's skin and protects the rhino from the diseases that can be carried by insects.

Fly swatter
(tail)

Hinge joints with large pistons for movement
(femur, tibia, and fibula with muscles attached)

Three extra-strong supports
(toes ending in rounded hooves)

Shock-absorbing pad
(flattened foot)

The rhino's legs end in flattened feet which together bear the animal's great weight. Each foot has three wide toes, each ending in a broad rounded hoof—the splayed-out toes and hooves spread the rhino's weight over a large area.

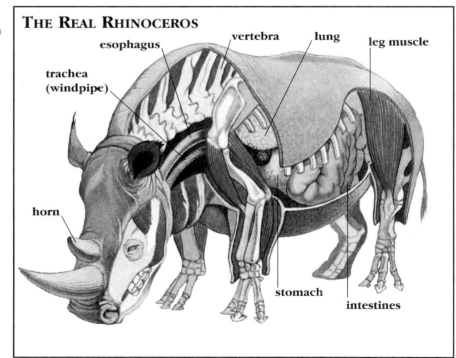

THE REAL RHINOCEROS

esophagus

vertebra

lung

leg muscle

trachea
(windpipe)

horn

stomach

intestines

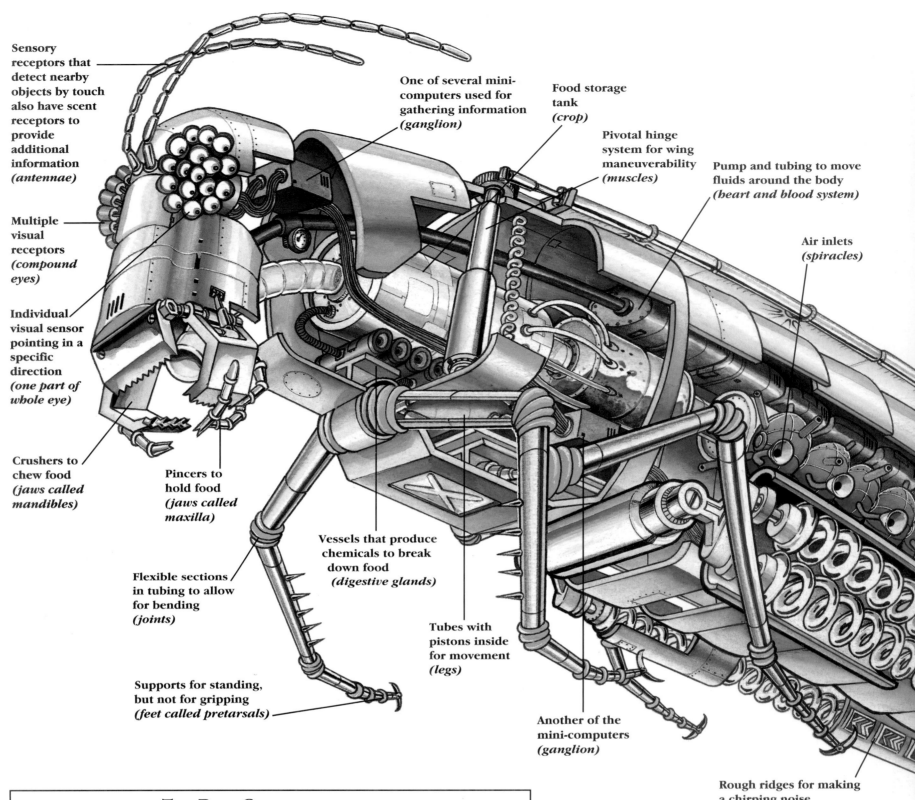

Sensory receptors that detect nearby objects by touch also have scent receptors to provide additional information *(antennae)*

One of several mini-computers used for gathering information *(ganglion)*

Food storage tank *(crop)*

Pivotal hinge system for wing maneuverability *(muscles)*

Pump and tubing to move fluids around the body *(heart and blood system)*

Air inlets *(spiracles)*

Multiple visual receptors *(compound eyes)*

Individual visual sensor pointing in a specific direction *(one part of whole eye)*

Crushers to chew food *(jaws called mandibles)*

Pincers to hold food *(jaws called maxilla)*

Vessels that produce chemicals to break down food *(digestive glands)*

Flexible sections in tubing to allow for bending *(joints)*

Tubes with pistons inside for movement *(legs)*

Supports for standing, but not for gripping *(feet called pretarsals)*

Another of the mini-computers *(ganglion)*

Rough ridges for making a chirping noise *(stridulatory pegs found on male grasshoppers)*

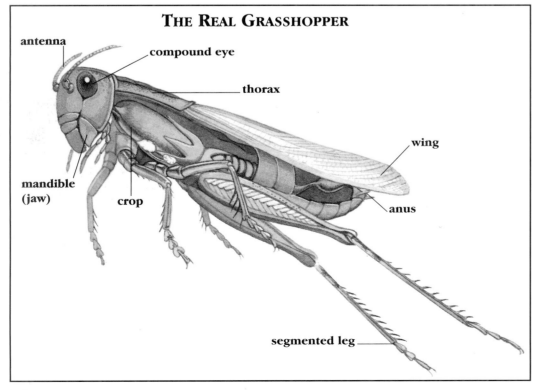

THE REAL GRASSHOPPER

antenna

compound eye

thorax

mandible (jaw)

crop

wing

anus

segmented leg

Inside the long rear section—the abdomen—is most of the intestine and the long heart. Insects such as the grasshopper do not have lungs. Instead, tubes (trachioles) connected to many openings (spiracles) take air from the outside directly to the tissues of the insects.

The grasshopper does not have a control center or brain like other animals. Its nervous system is connected to various bundles of nerves around the body called ganglia.

Grasshopper

A grasshopper is an insect that lives in and feeds on grass and other plants. Using huge hind legs, the grasshopper makes gigantic leaps into the air. After its spring-assisted takeoff, it can unfurl its two pairs of wings and continue flying with them.

Like all insects, the grasshopper has six legs. The two rear legs are specialized and strengthened for jumping, while the front two pairs are used only for walking on the ground. The grasshopper's head has two antennae that are able to feel and smell what is nearby. It also has two compound eyes that are made up of hundreds of individual eyelets. Each eyelet, called an ommatidium, has its own lens and light-sensitive cells, and together they provide an overall picture of a wide area surrounding the grasshopper. The mouthparts are a set of movable jaws that let the grasshopper chomp its way through grass blades.

GRASSHOPPER FACTS
Country: worldwide
Habitat: found on the ground and on vegetation; the majority of grasshoppers live in meadows, fields, and hedges
Length: up to 3 in. (8 cm), but mostly ⅝–1⅛ in. (15–30 mm)
Closest relatives: walkingstick and cricket

Actual size

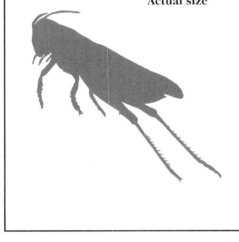

Flight enablers
(wings that can be unfurled for flight)

Waste disposal unit
(anus)

Hinge joints allow legs to bend
(knees)

Massive springs used to launch into the jump
(muscles)

Like all insects, the grasshopper has a body divided into three sections—the head, the thorax, and the abdomen. The large abdomen is made of ten overlapping sections, each with a spiracle (a breathing hole) on either side of the body. These sections can move against each other, which makes the abdomen flexible.

Look carefully at the upper part of the back legs and you will see another special feature of the male grasshopper. There are file-like ridges on the inner sides of the legs. They can be rubbed against the side of the robot's body to make a loud rasping noise to signal to other grasshopper robots. Living male grasshoppers make their chirping songs in the same way. They do this to attract females and to mark their territory.

The main jumping legs are multi-jointed and contain long and powerful springs. They can be compressed before a jump and then suddenly released to throw the robot into the air. Once in the air, the grasshopper uses its wings to fly.

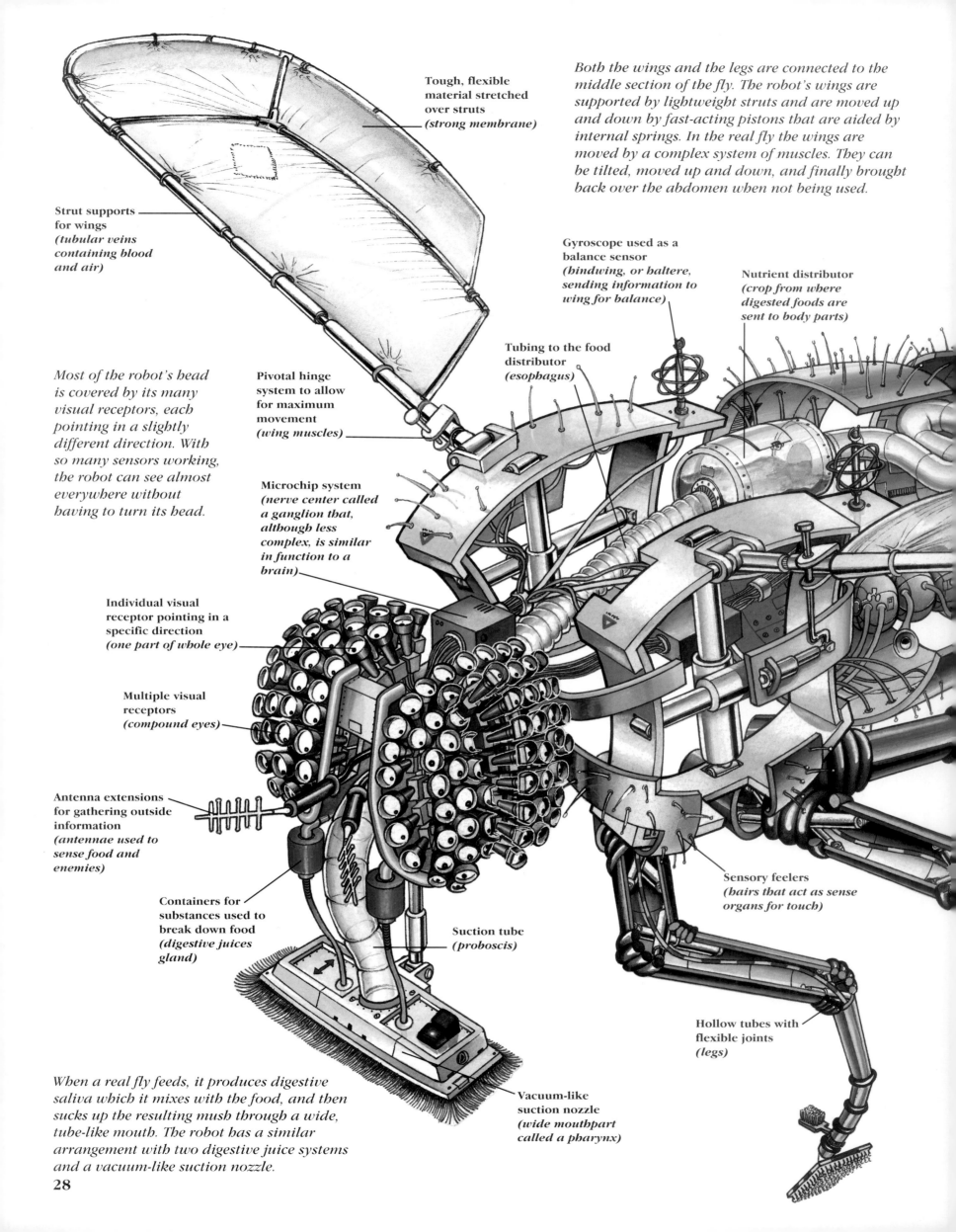

Tough, flexible material stretched over struts
(strong membrane)

Both the wings and the legs are connected to the middle section of the fly. The robot's wings are supported by lightweight struts and are moved up and down by fast-acting pistons that are aided by internal springs. In the real fly the wings are moved by a complex system of muscles. They can be tilted, moved up and down, and finally brought back over the abdomen when not being used.

Strut supports for wings
(tubular veins containing blood and air)

Gyroscope used as a balance sensor
(hindwing, or haltere, sending information to wing for balance)

Nutrient distributor
(crop from where digested foods are sent to body parts)

Most of the robot's head is covered by its many visual receptors, each pointing in a slightly different direction. With so many sensors working, the robot can see almost everywhere without having to turn its head.

Pivotal hinge system to allow for maximum movement
(wing muscles)

Tubing to the food distributor
(esophagus)

Microchip system
(nerve center called a ganglion that, although less complex, is similar in function to a brain)

Individual visual receptor pointing in a specific direction
(one part of whole eye)

Multiple visual receptors
(compound eyes)

Antenna extensions for gathering outside information
(antennae used to sense food and enemies)

Containers for substances used to break down food
(digestive juices gland)

Suction tube
(proboscis)

Sensory feelers
(hairs that act as sense organs for touch)

Hollow tubes with flexible joints
(legs)

When a real fly feeds, it produces digestive saliva which it mixes with the food, and then sucks up the resulting mush through a wide, tube-like mouth. The robot has a similar arrangement with two digestive juice systems and a vacuum-like suction nozzle.

Vacuum-like suction nozzle
(wide mouthpart called a pharynx)

28

House Fly

Waste disposal tubing *(intestines)*

Rigid outer casing for support and shape *(exoskeleton)*

Air inlets *(spiracles)*

Sensory pads with hooked endings for extra grip *(clinging feet with taste organs on them)*

Cleaning brush used for grooming *(bristles on inside of legs)*

Try to catch a fly and you will find out just how fast it can move. With huge compound eyes that are made up of hundreds of separate eyelets, the fly sees your hand coming. With a buzz of fast-beating wings, it is gone before you can touch it.

Although only the size of an adult's fingernail, the fly is an amazingly complicated animal. Its body is made up of three sections. The head contains the eyes and mouth. The mid-section, or thorax, has three pairs of many-jointed legs and a pair of wings. A hind section, the abdomen, holds all the other body organs. Most of the body is covered in tiny hairs that let the fly detect pressure and vibrations. There is no skeleton inside a fly. Instead, the outer skin of the body, called the cuticle, is stiff and shell-like and forms a type of outer skeleton, or exoskeleton. This robot fly is built in a similar way with a rigid casing on each of its sections.

FLY FACTS
Country: worldwide
Habitat: everywhere except extreme climates
Length: around ½ in. (1 cm)
Weight: almost nothing
Closest relatives: mosquitoes and horseflies

Actual size

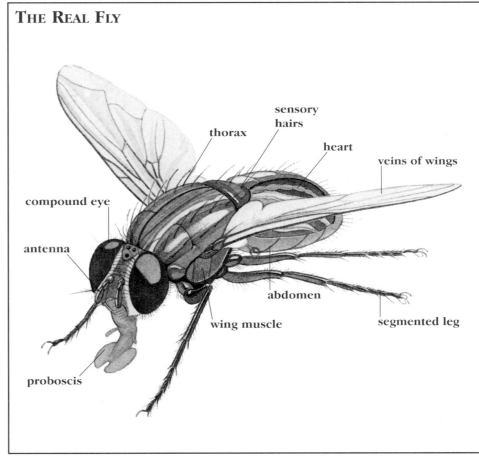

THE REAL FLY

sensory hairs

thorax

heart

veins of wings

compound eye

antenna

abdomen

wing muscle

segmented leg

proboscis

29

Giant Squid

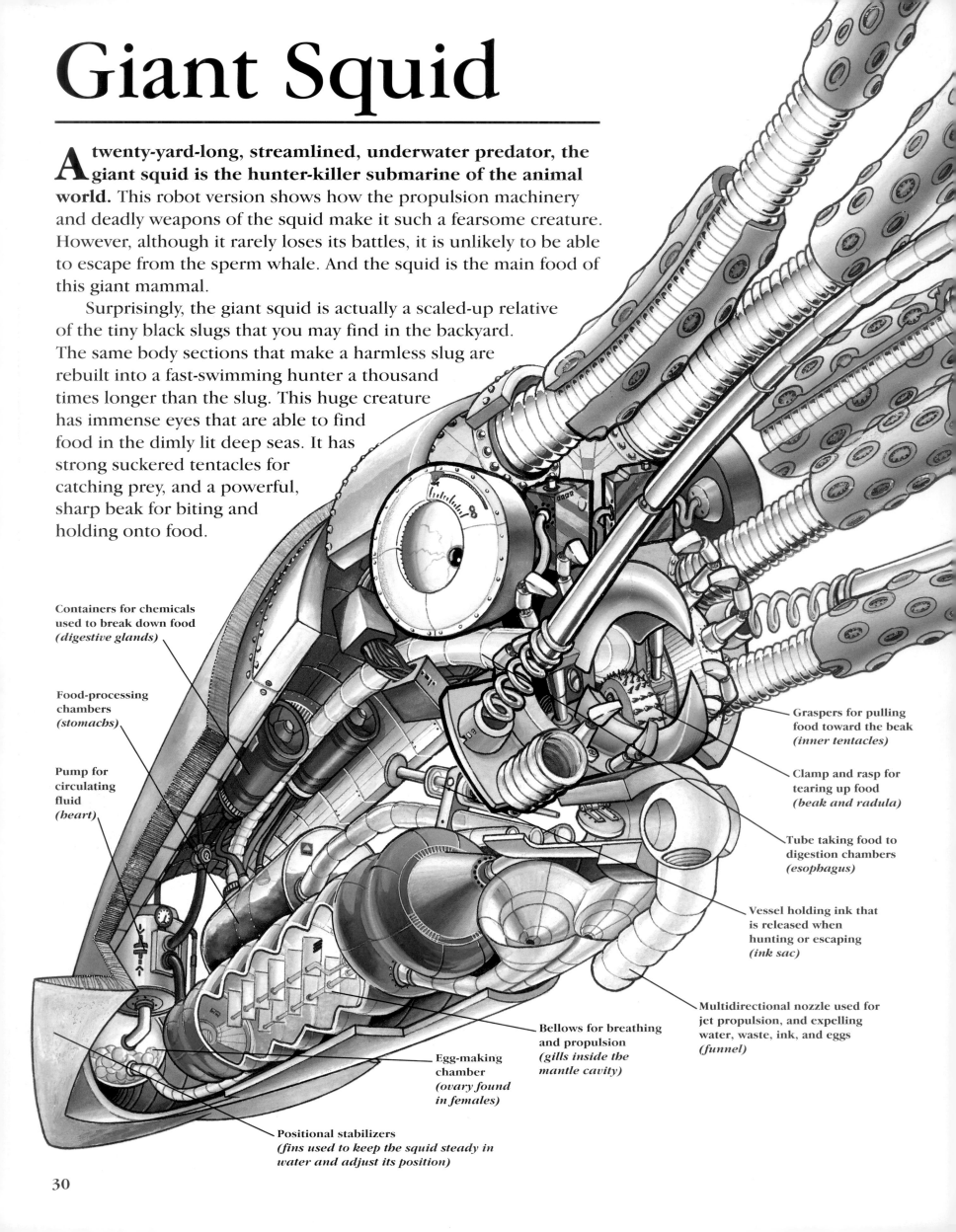

A twenty-yard-long, streamlined, underwater predator, the giant squid is the hunter-killer submarine of the animal world. This robot version shows how the propulsion machinery and deadly weapons of the squid make it such a fearsome creature. However, although it rarely loses its battles, it is unlikely to be able to escape from the sperm whale. And the squid is the main food of this giant mammal.

Surprisingly, the giant squid is actually a scaled-up relative of the tiny black slugs that you may find in the backyard. The same body sections that make a harmless slug are rebuilt into a fast-swimming hunter a thousand times longer than the slug. This huge creature has immense eyes that are able to find food in the dimly lit deep seas. It has strong suckered tentacles for catching prey, and a powerful, sharp beak for biting and holding onto food.

Containers for chemicals used to break down food *(digestive glands)*

Food-processing chambers *(stomachs)*

Pump for circulating fluid *(heart)*

Graspers for pulling food toward the beak *(inner tentacles)*

Clamp and rasp for tearing up food *(beak and radula)*

Tube taking food to digestion chambers *(esophagus)*

Vessel holding ink that is released when hunting or escaping *(ink sac)*

Multidirectional nozzle used for jet propulsion, and expelling water, waste, ink, and eggs *(funnel)*

Bellows for breathing and propulsion *(gills inside the mantle cavity)*

Egg-making chamber *(ovary found in females)*

Positional stabilizers *(fins used to keep the squid steady in water and adjust its position)*

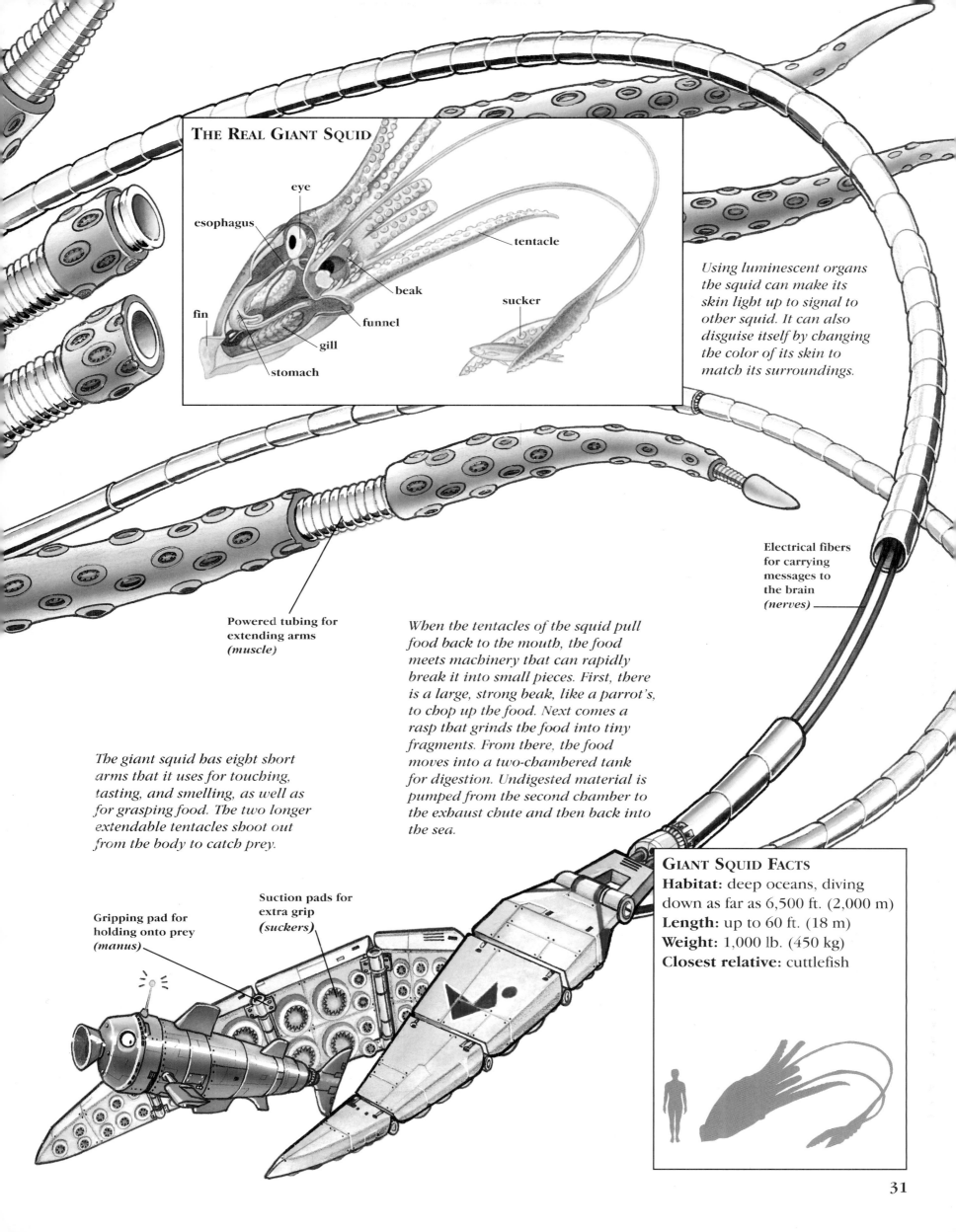

THE REAL GIANT SQUID

eye

esophagus

beak

tentacle

fin

funnel

sucker

gill

stomach

Using luminescent organs the squid can make its skin light up to signal to other squid. It can also disguise itself by changing the color of its skin to match its surroundings.

Powered tubing for extending arms *(muscle)*

Electrical fibers for carrying messages to the brain *(nerves)*

When the tentacles of the squid pull food back to the mouth, the food meets machinery that can rapidly break it into small pieces. First, there is a large, strong beak, like a parrot's, to chop up the food. Next comes a rasp that grinds the food into tiny fragments. From there, the food moves into a two-chambered tank for digestion. Undigested material is pumped from the second chamber to the exhaust chute and then back into the sea.

The giant squid has eight short arms that it uses for touching, tasting, and smelling, as well as for grasping food. The two longer extendable tentacles shoot out from the body to catch prey.

Suction pads for extra grip *(suckers)*

Gripping pad for holding onto prey *(manus)*

GIANT SQUID FACTS
Habitat: deep oceans, diving down as far as 6,500 ft. (2,000 m)
Length: up to 60 ft. (18 m)
Weight: 1,000 lb. (450 kg)
Closest relative: cuttlefish

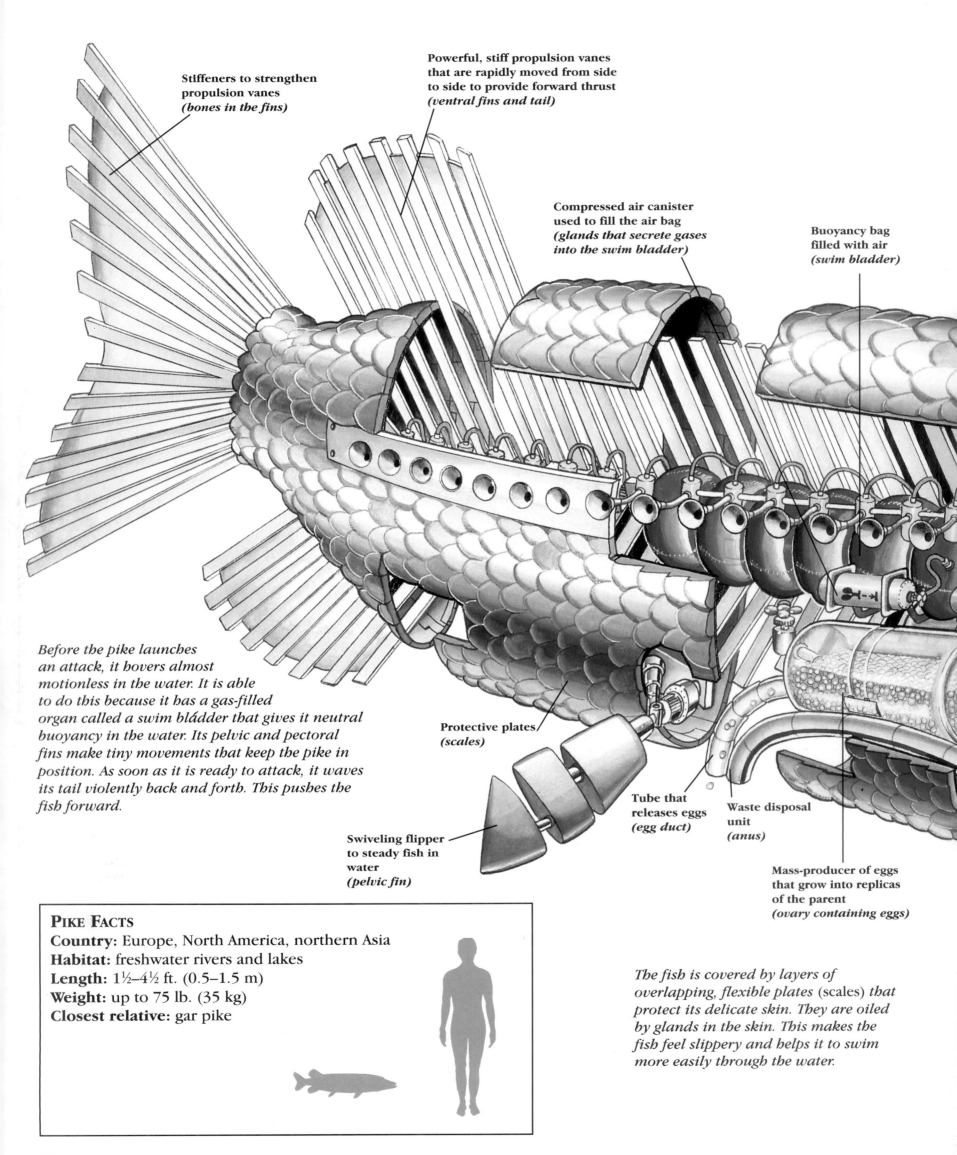

Stiffeners to strengthen propulsion vanes
(bones in the fins)

Powerful, stiff propulsion vanes that are rapidly moved from side to side to provide forward thrust
(ventral fins and tail)

Compressed air canister used to fill the air bag
(glands that secrete gases into the swim bladder)

Buoyancy bag filled with air
(swim bladder)

Before the pike launches an attack, it hovers almost motionless in the water. It is able to do this because it has a gas-filled organ called a swim bládder that gives it neutral buoyancy in the water. Its pelvic and pectoral fins make tiny movements that keep the pike in position. As soon as it is ready to attack, it waves its tail violently back and forth. This pushes the fish forward.

Protective plates
(scales)

Swiveling flipper to steady fish in water
(pelvic fin)

Tube that releases eggs
(egg duct)

Waste disposal unit
(anus)

Mass-producer of eggs that grow into replicas of the parent
(ovary containing eggs)

PIKE FACTS
Country: Europe, North America, northern Asia
Habitat: freshwater rivers and lakes
Length: 1½–4½ ft. (0.5–1.5 m)
Weight: up to 75 lb. (35 kg)
Closest relative: gar pike

The fish is covered by layers of overlapping, flexible plates (scales) that protect its delicate skin. They are oiled by glands in the skin. This makes the fish feel slippery and helps it to swim more easily through the water.

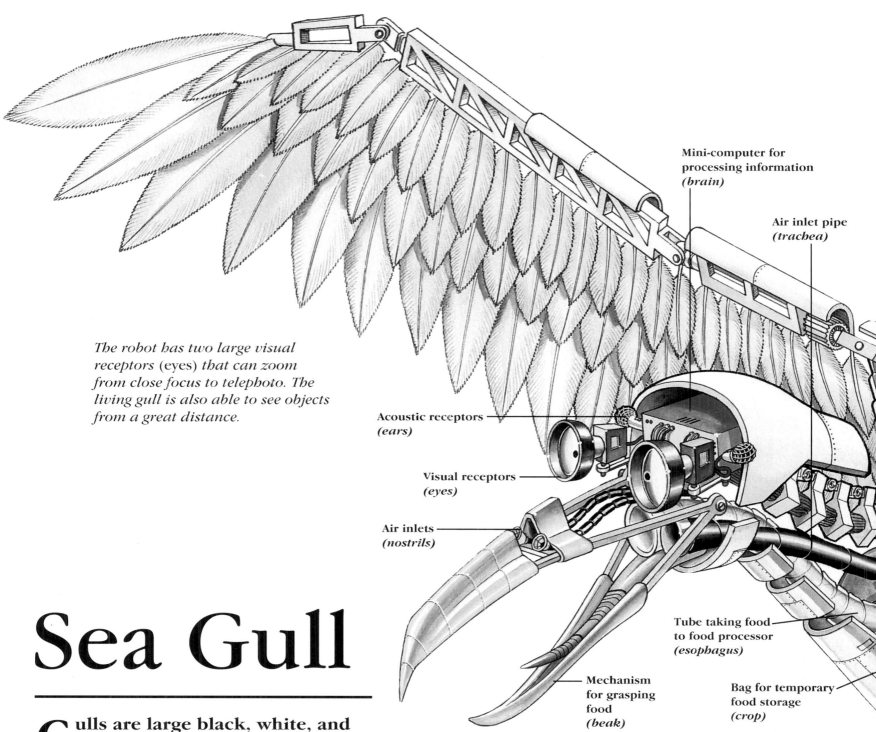

Mini-computer for
processing information
(brain)

Air inlet pipe
(trachea)

*The robot has two large visual
receptors* (eyes) *that can zoom
from close focus to telephoto. The
living gull is also able to see objects
from a great distance.*

Acoustic receptors
(ears)

Visual receptors
(eyes)

Air inlets
(nostrils)

Tube taking food
to food processor
(esophagus)

Mechanism
for grasping
food
(beak)

Bag for temporary
food storage
(crop)

Sea Gull

Gulls are large black, white, and
**gray seabirds that usually live and nest near
the coastline.** They feed on live and dead prey that they
find at the water's edge or in the sea. Gulls pick up this
food—fish, shellfish, and worms—using their strong
beaks. The hook at the end of the beak helps the bird
keep a grip on its prey.

The gull can walk on land, swim in the sea, and fly
through the air because of the special design of its
feathers, bones, wings, and feet. The feathers and bones
are lightweight, which means that when flapping its
wings, the bird can lift itself off the ground. The feathers
are also waterproof, so when the bird sits on water, it
floats. The bird's slightly clawed feet can grip the ground
as well as propel it through water. The webbing between
the bird's claws acts in a similar way to flippers you might
wear when swimming.

*The upper and lower sections of
the robot's beak are made of an
inner framework* (jawbones)
covered with an outer layer
(tough beak sheath).

Pike

A **pike is a sleek and speedy predatory fish that lives in freshwater rivers and lakes**. When hunting, it hovers among water weeds until it sees a smaller fish swimming past. Then, with tremendous acceleration, it speeds forward to catch the fish in its sharp-toothed jaws.

The pike finds its prey with its large eyes, which look forward along grooves in the front part of the upper jaw. It can also sense water vibrations. These are received through a line of tiny openings along each side of the fish called the lateral line. Minute sensors inside these openings, or pores, can perceive very slight movements in the water and give clues as to where the prey might be. A third sense used when finding prey is smell. The forward-pointing nostrils of the pike pick up chemical clues from the surrounding waters.

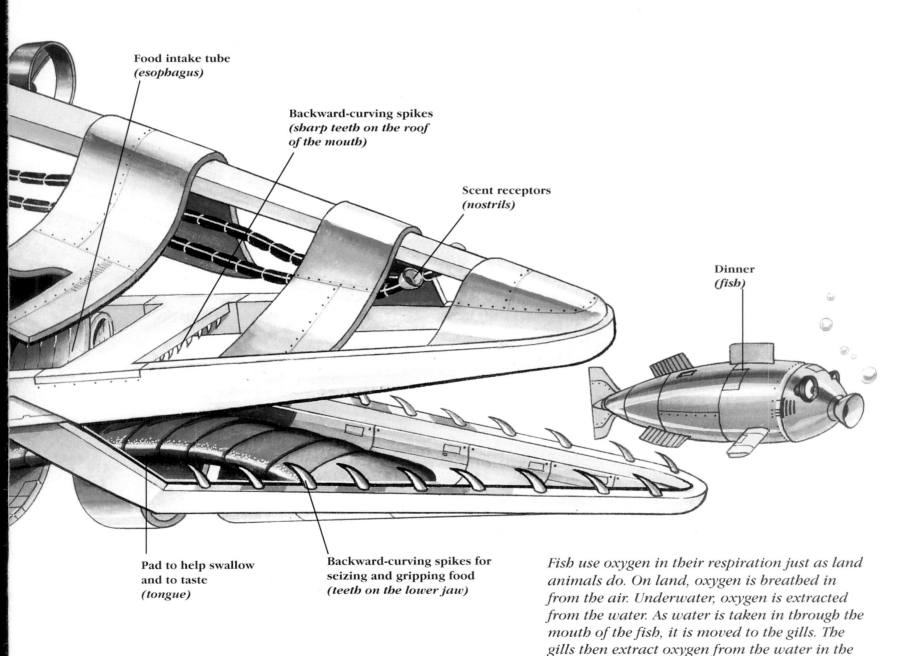

Food intake tube
(esophagus)

Backward-curving spikes
*(sharp teeth on the roof
of the mouth)*

Scent receptors
(nostrils)

Dinner
(fish)

Pad to help swallow
and to taste
(tongue)

Backward-curving spikes for
seizing and gripping food
(teeth on the lower jaw)

Fish use oxygen in their respiration just as land animals do. On land, oxygen is breathed in from the air. Underwater, oxygen is extracted from the water. As water is taken in through the mouth of the fish, it is moved to the gills. The gills then extract oxygen from the water in the same way that lungs take oxygen from the air.

34

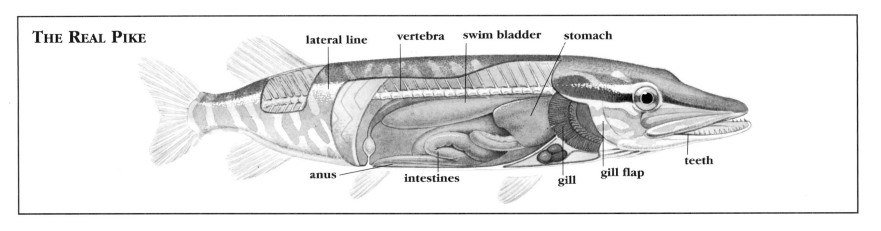

THE REAL PIKE

lateral line • vertebra • swim bladder • stomach • teeth • gill flap • gill • intestines • anus

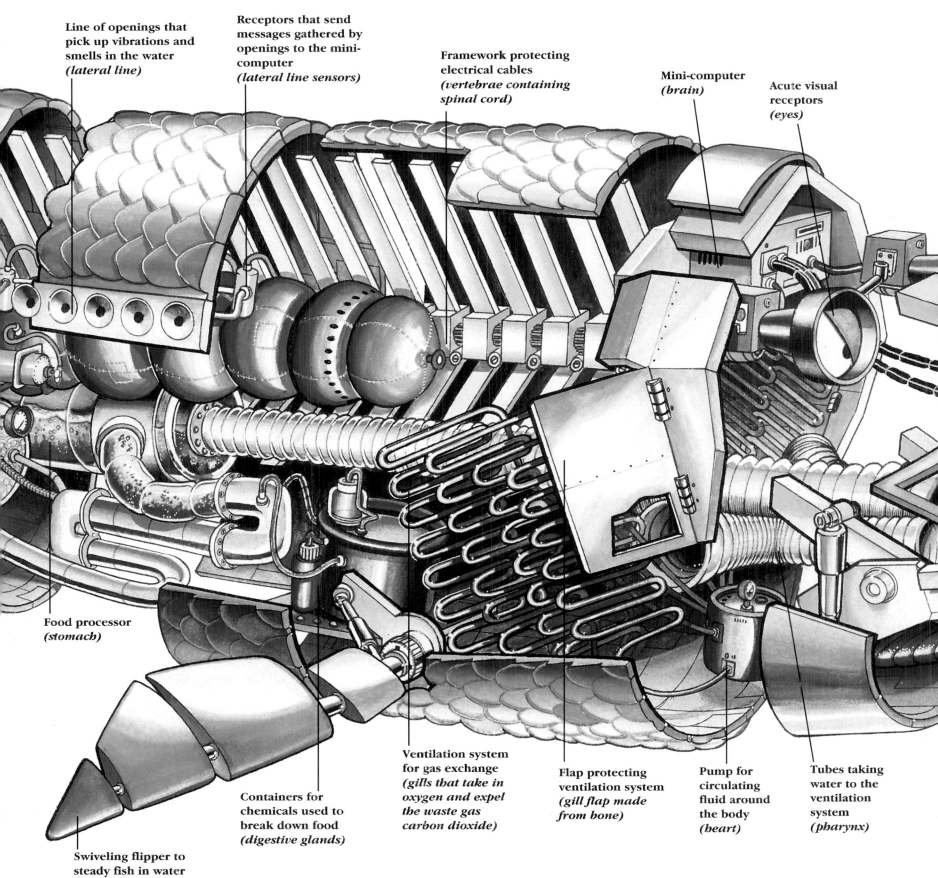

Line of openings that pick up vibrations and smells in the water *(lateral line)*

Receptors that send messages gathered by openings to the mini-computer *(lateral line sensors)*

Framework protecting electrical cables *(vertebrae containing spinal cord)*

Mini-computer *(brain)*

Acute visual receptors *(eyes)*

Food processor *(stomach)*

Swiveling flipper to steady fish in water *(pectoral fin)*

Containers for chemicals used to break down food *(digestive glands)*

Ventilation system for gas exchange *(gills that take in oxygen and expel the waste gas carbon dioxide)*

Flap protecting ventilation system *(gill flap made from bone)*

Pump for circulating fluid around the body *(heart)*

Tubes taking water to the ventilation system *(pharynx)*

All birds have a special breathing system that allows them to utilize oxygen more efficiently than mammals can. Air goes in through the trachea to the lungs, then out of the lungs to air sacs. The air sacs act like bellows, alternately drawing air in and pushing it back out to the lungs, where more oxygen can be taken from it. This process helps to give the bird the energy it needs for flight.

Birds have digestive pouches that perform separate tasks. When the bird swallows a fish, the food goes down the esophagus into the crop where it can be stored until the bird is ready to digest it. It will then go to the gizzard, which grinds it with stones that the bird has swallowed especially for this purpose. In the stomach and intestines, the nutrients are separated from the waste and distributed throughout the body.

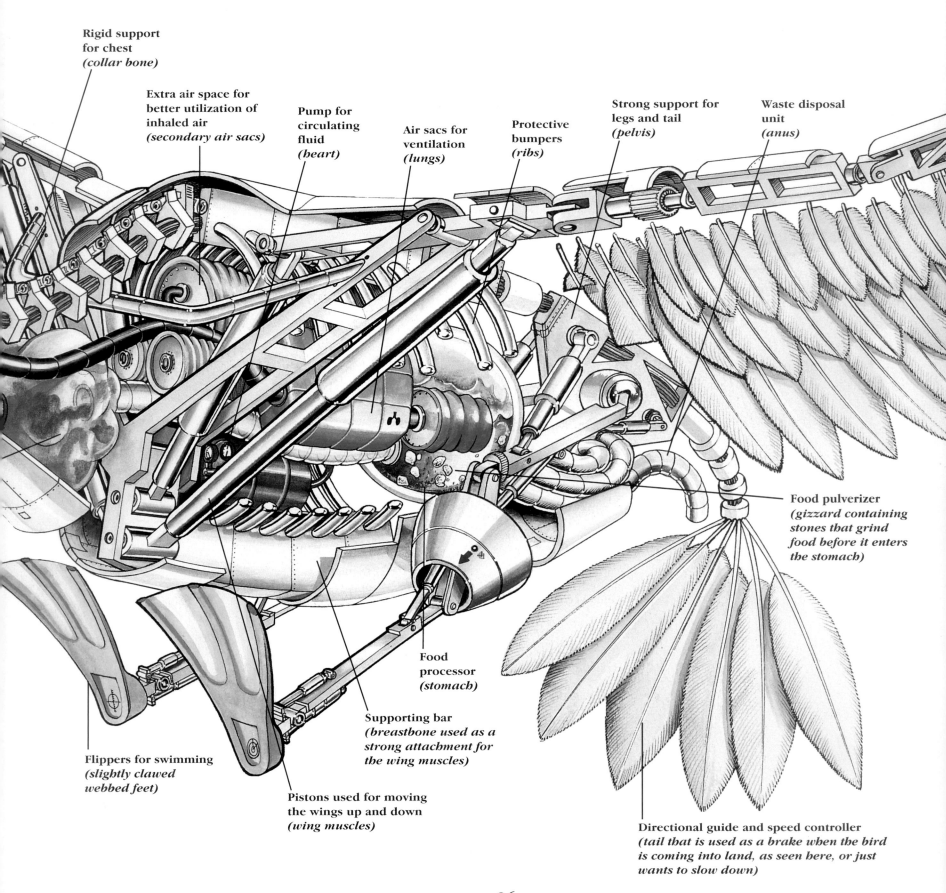

Rigid support
for chest
(collar bone)

Extra air space for
better utilization of
inhaled air
(secondary air sacs)

Pump for
circulating
fluid
(heart)

Air sacs for
ventilation
(lungs)

Protective
bumpers
(ribs)

Strong support for
legs and tail
(pelvis)

Waste disposal
unit
(anus)

Food pulverizer
*(gizzard containing
stones that grind
food before it enters
the stomach)*

Flippers for swimming
*(slightly clawed
webbed feet)*

Food
processor
(stomach)

Supporting bar
*(breastbone used as a
strong attachment for
the wing muscles)*

Pistons used for moving
the wings up and down
(wing muscles)

Directional guide and speed controller
*(tail that is used as a brake when the bird
is coming into land, as seen here, or just
wants to slow down)*

36

The leading edge of each wing is made of a long, hinged, hollow spar (bone). Attached to this are rows of overlapping vanes (flight feathers) *that make up the main area of the wing. The wing structures provide lift and thrust for flight. They can be held out straight for gliding and soaring, or they can beat up and down, powered by the huge flight pistons* (flight muscles).

GULL FACTS
Country: worldwide
Habitat: coastlines
Wingspan: 24–63 in. (0.6–1.6 m)
Weight: up to about 4½ lb. (2 kg)
Closest relative: albatross

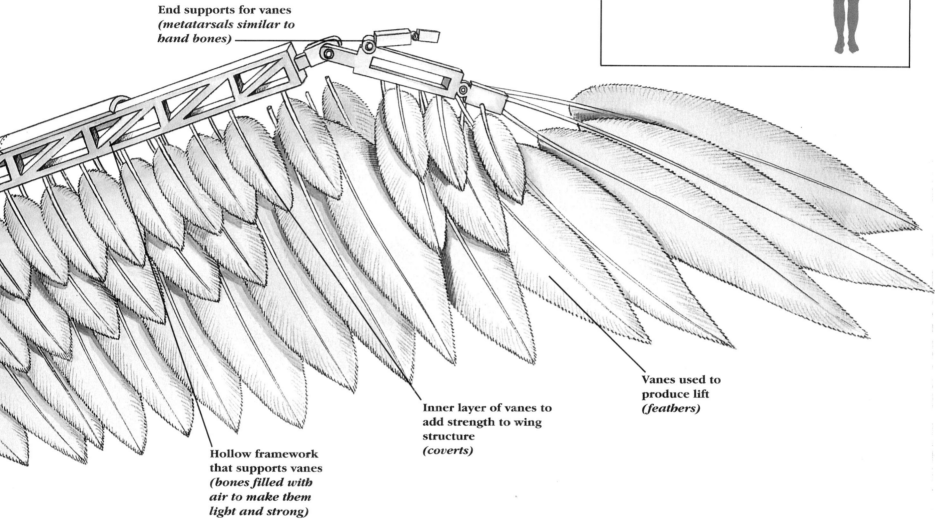

End supports for vanes *(metatarsals similar to hand bones)*

Vanes used to produce lift *(feathers)*

Inner layer of vanes to add strength to wing structure *(coverts)*

Hollow framework that supports vanes *(bones filled with air to make them light and strong)*

THE REAL GULL

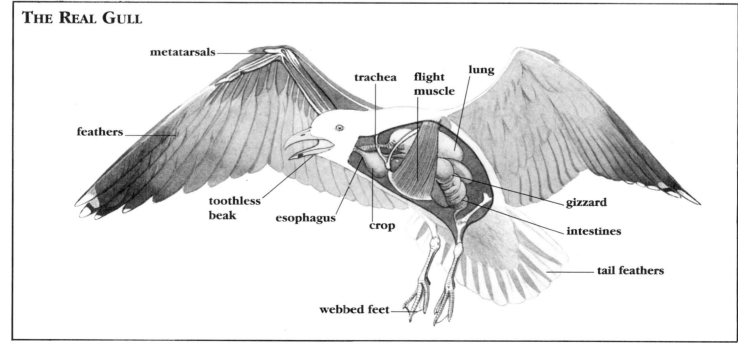

metatarsals

trachea

flight muscle

lung

feathers

toothless beak

esophagus

crop

gizzard

intestines

tail feathers

webbed feet

As in the real animal, the robot's mouth is beak-shaped and toothless. The sharp edges of the beak are used to grab and cut up pieces of green grass or leaves that are then swallowed.

Protective helmet
(fused bones of the skull)

Visual sensor
(eye)

Vents connected to the air intake pipe
(nostrils)

The tortoise's skull is made of strong bones that are fused together to form a tough, helmet-like casing. It shields the brain inside, just as the shell protects the animal's other soft organs.

Electrical fibers
(spinal cord inside spinal column)

Tube to take food to processor
(esophagus)

Air intake pipe
(trachea)

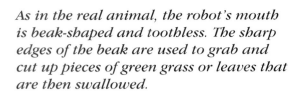

Tortoise

uilt like an armored car, the tortoise is a long-necked reptile. A reptile is a cold-blooded animal that lays eggs. Because it is cold-blooded, the tortoise has to live in warm climates, so that it never runs out of energy. If the weather became too cold, the tortoise would start to get sluggish because its body temperature would not be high enough for it to function properly.

Although tortoises may seem clumsy and slow and therefore vulnerable, they can live for more then 70 years. In fact the design of the tortoise has been so successful that the species has remained virtually unchanged for more than 65 million years.

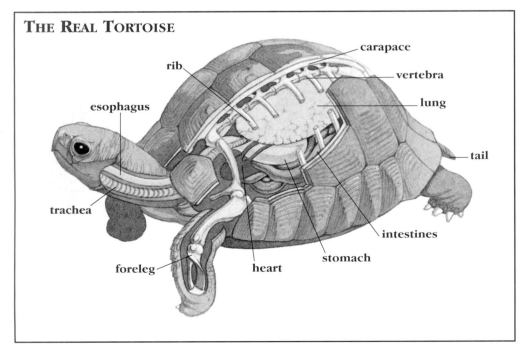

THE REAL TORTOISE

carapace

rib

vertebra

esophagus

lung

tail

trachea

foreleg

heart

stomach

intestines

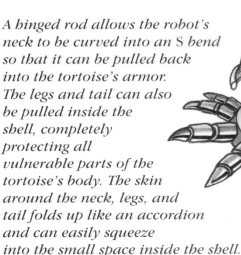

A hinged rod allows the robot's neck to be curved into an S bend so that it can be pulled back into the tortoise's armor. The legs and tail can also be pulled inside the shell, completely protecting all vulnerable parts of the tortoise's body. The skin around the neck, legs, and tail folds up like an accordion and can easily squeeze into the small space inside the shell.

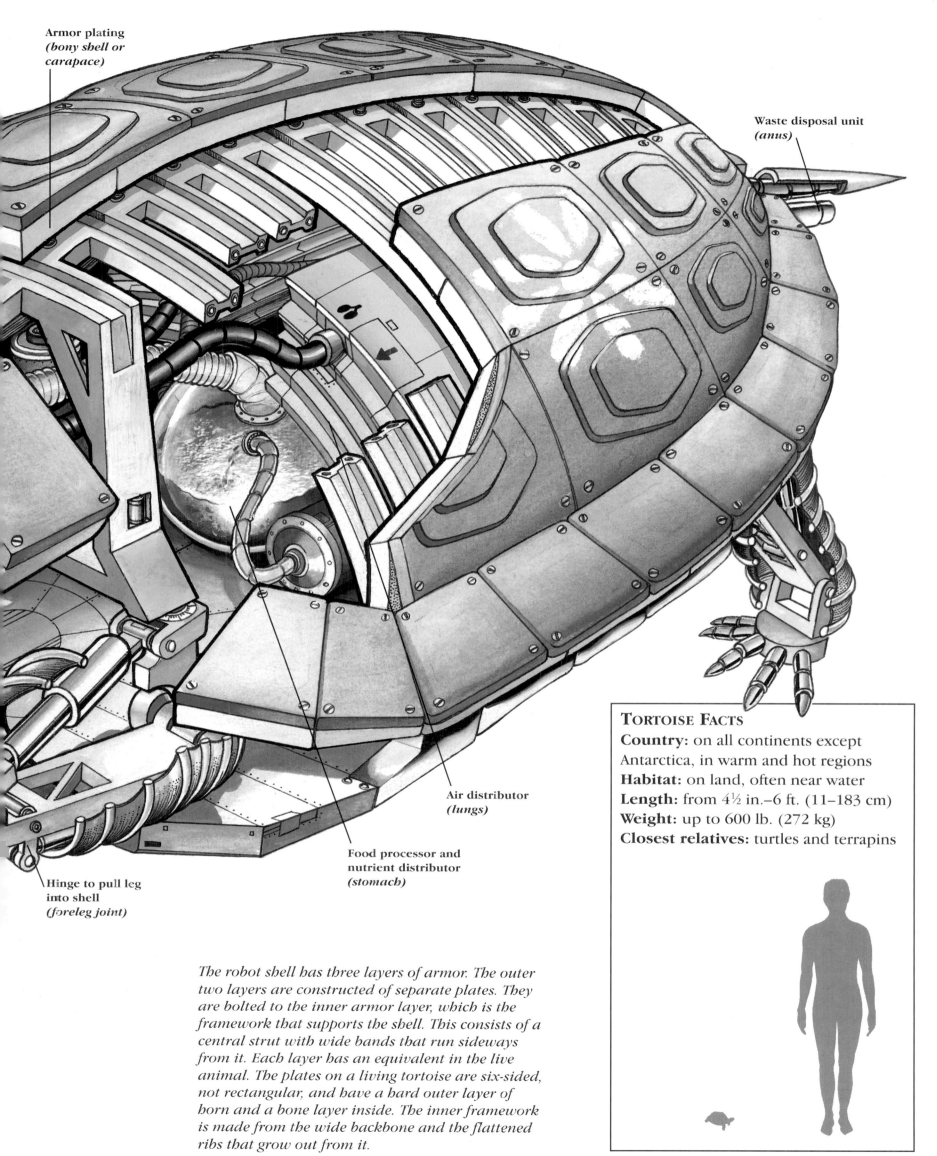

Armor plating
*(bony shell or
carapace)*

Waste disposal unit
(anus)

Air distributor
(lungs)

Food processor and
nutrient distributor
(stomach)

Hinge to pull leg
into shell
(foreleg joint)

TORTOISE FACTS
Country: on all continents except
Antarctica, in warm and hot regions
Habitat: on land, often near water
Length: from 4½ in.–6 ft. (11–183 cm)
Weight: up to 600 lb. (272 kg)
Closest relatives: turtles and terrapins

*The robot shell has three layers of armor. The outer
two layers are constructed of separate plates. They
are bolted to the inner armor layer, which is the
framework that supports the shell. This consists of a
central strut with wide bands that run sideways
from it. Each layer has an equivalent in the live
animal. The plates on a living tortoise are six-sided,
not rectangular, and have a hard outer layer of
horn and a bone layer inside. The inner framework
is made from the wide backbone and the flattened
ribs that grow out from it.*

Mussel

Mussels live on or near the seashore where saltwater tides go in and out. At low tide, you will find mussels by the thousands stuck tightly to rocks, harbor walls, and wooden pilings. When you see them out of water, you will see only tightly shut blue-black shells. The animal inside the shell cannot be seen. Only when the tide is in and the mussel is underwater does the animal show itself.

Mussels belong to a group of animals known as mollusks. These are invertebrate animals that have soft bodies, usually enclosed within a hard shell. Snails and slugs are also mollusks. The mussel is a bivalve, which means the animal is surrounded by two connected shells.

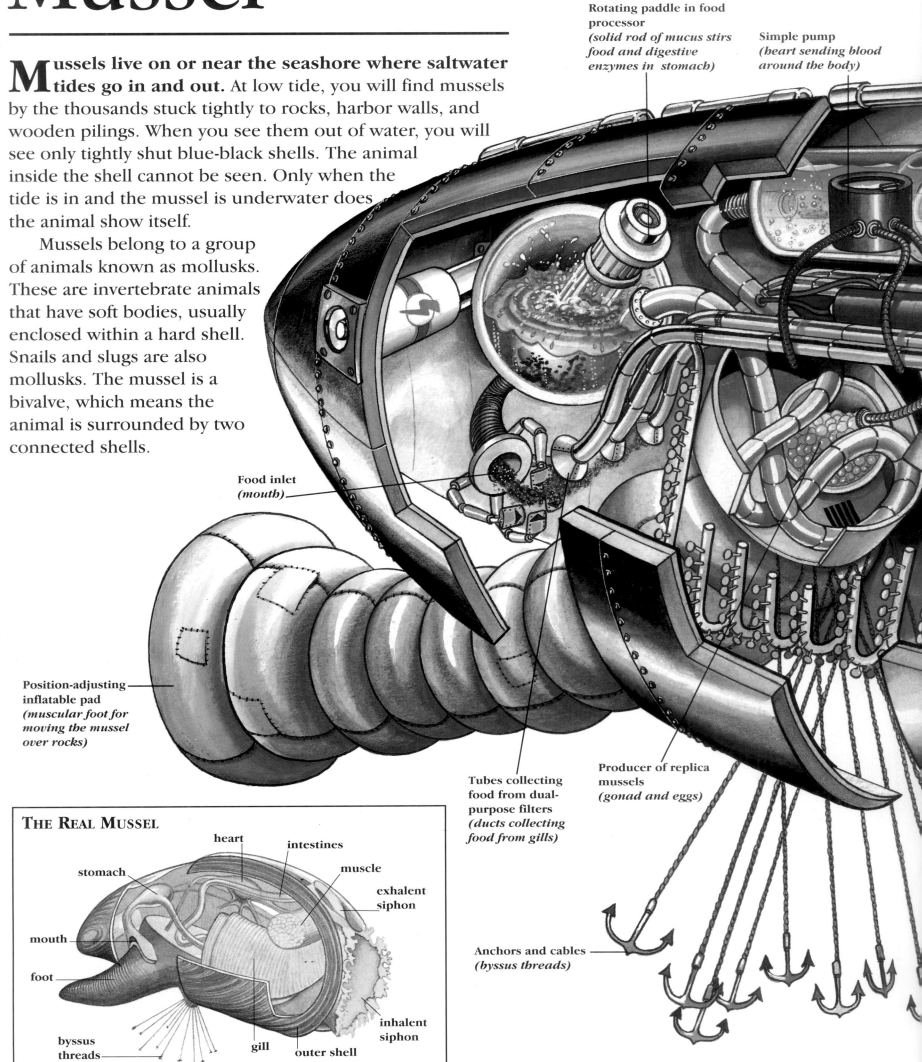

Rotating paddle in food processor
(solid rod of mucus stirs food and digestive enzymes in stomach)

Simple pump
(heart sending blood around the body)

Food inlet
(mouth)

Position-adjusting inflatable pad
(muscular foot for moving the mussel over rocks)

Tubes collecting food from dual-purpose filters
(ducts collecting food from gills)

Producer of replica mussels
(gonad and eggs)

Anchors and cables
(byssus threads)

THE REAL MUSSEL

heart

intestines

stomach

muscle

exhalent siphon

mouth

foot

inhalent siphon

byssus threads

gill

outer shell

40

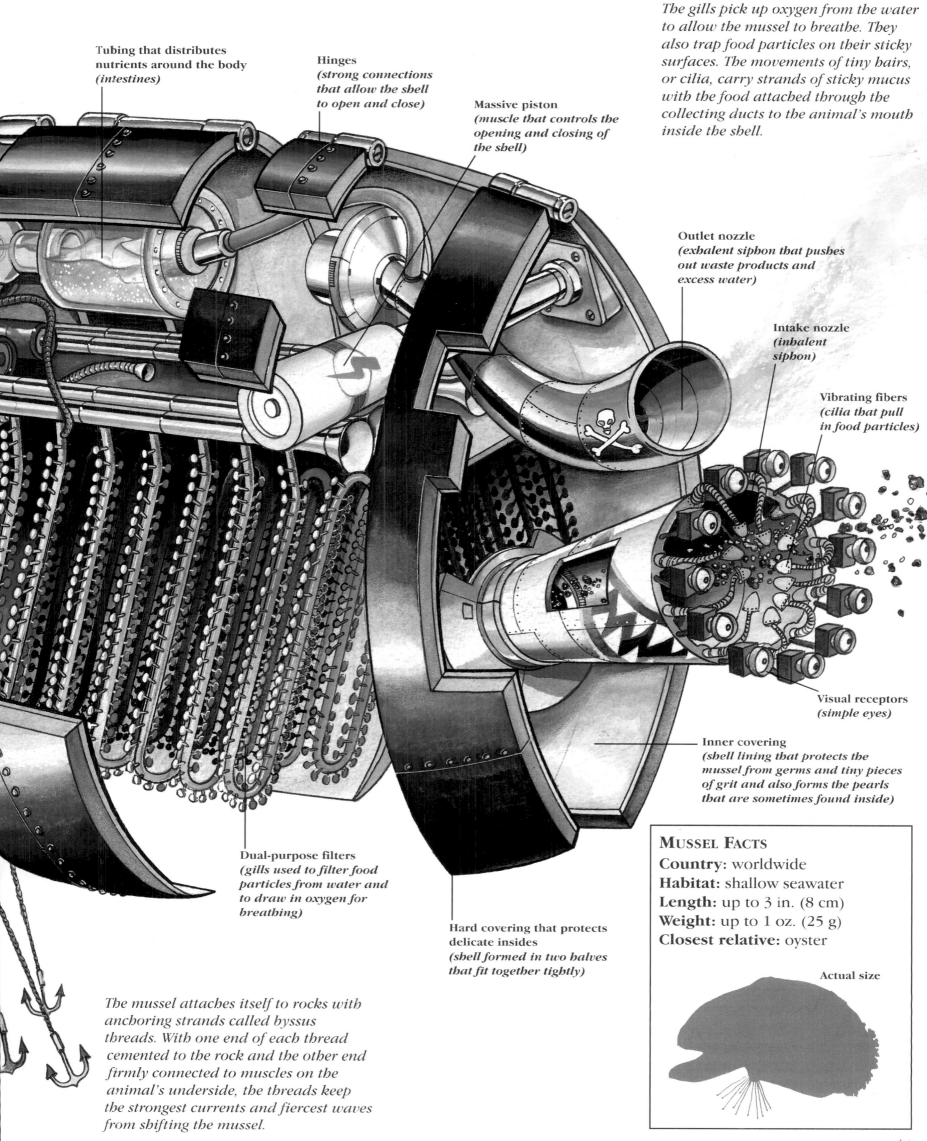

Tubing that distributes
nutrients around the body
(intestines)

Hinges
(strong connections
that allow the shell
to open and close)

Massive piston
(muscle that controls the
opening and closing of
the shell)

The gills pick up oxygen from the water
to allow the mussel to breathe. They
also trap food particles on their sticky
surfaces. The movements of tiny hairs,
or cilia, carry strands of sticky mucus
with the food attached through the
collecting ducts to the animal's mouth
inside the shell.

Outlet nozzle
(exhalent siphon that pushes
out waste products and
excess water)

Intake nozzle
(inhalent
siphon)

Vibrating fibers
(cilia that pull
in food particles)

Visual receptors
(simple eyes)

Inner covering
(shell lining that protects the
mussel from germs and tiny pieces
of grit and also forms the pearls
that are sometimes found inside)

Dual-purpose filters
(gills used to filter food
particles from water and
to draw in oxygen for
breathing)

Hard covering that protects
delicate insides
(shell formed in two halves
that fit together tightly)

MUSSEL FACTS
Country: worldwide
Habitat: shallow seawater
Length: up to 3 in. (8 cm)
Weight: up to 1 oz. (25 g)
Closest relative: oyster

Actual size

The mussel attaches itself to rocks with
anchoring strands called byssus
threads. With one end of each thread
cemented to the rock and the other end
firmly connected to muscles on the
animal's underside, the threads keep
the strongest currents and fiercest waves
from shifting the mussel.

41

T4 Virus

Viruses are the smallest living organisms. You cannot see a virus with a normal microscope—it is only with a high-powered instrument called an electron microscope that scientists have been able to observe these amazingly small beings. It is difficult to imagine that viruses are alive because they do not feed or breathe. However, they do reproduce—something that all living creatures do—but require the help of their victims to accomplish this.

Each type of virus infects a different form of life. There are some, for example, that only cause damage to mushrooms; others cause diseases in insects or in the plants we grow for food. Many human diseases are the result of infections from viruses. Serious viral diseases include influenza, chicken pox, and AIDS.

Even the large germs called bacteria have their own viral diseases. These are caused by viruses that have tails that allow them to penetrate the bacterial cell. One of these is the T4 virus.

A virus consists of two parts. The first part is a protective coat. The second, inside the coat, is a set of virus genes, making up a coiled string of DNA. Genes and DNA are the basic building blocks for all life. They control how all living things are put together.

A good way to think of what genes are is to liken DNA to a story. Every word of that story is a gene. If you put the words together in one order, they result in one particular story. Put them another way and the story changes. In the robot virus, the floppy disks are the words and the story is the coiled strand of DNA.

Pirate flag
(although this has no equivalent on the virus, it shows that the virus enters a bacterium and kills it!)

Floppy disk
(gene storing information about the make-up of the virus)

String tying all the floppy disks together
(coiled DNA molecule)

Strong outer layer
(protective coat arranged in six-sided crystalline shapes)

String of floppy disks ready to inject into target
(thread of DNA molecule ready to enter bacterium)

Extended spring
(coil that compresses upon landing)

Landing struts
(stabilizing legs)

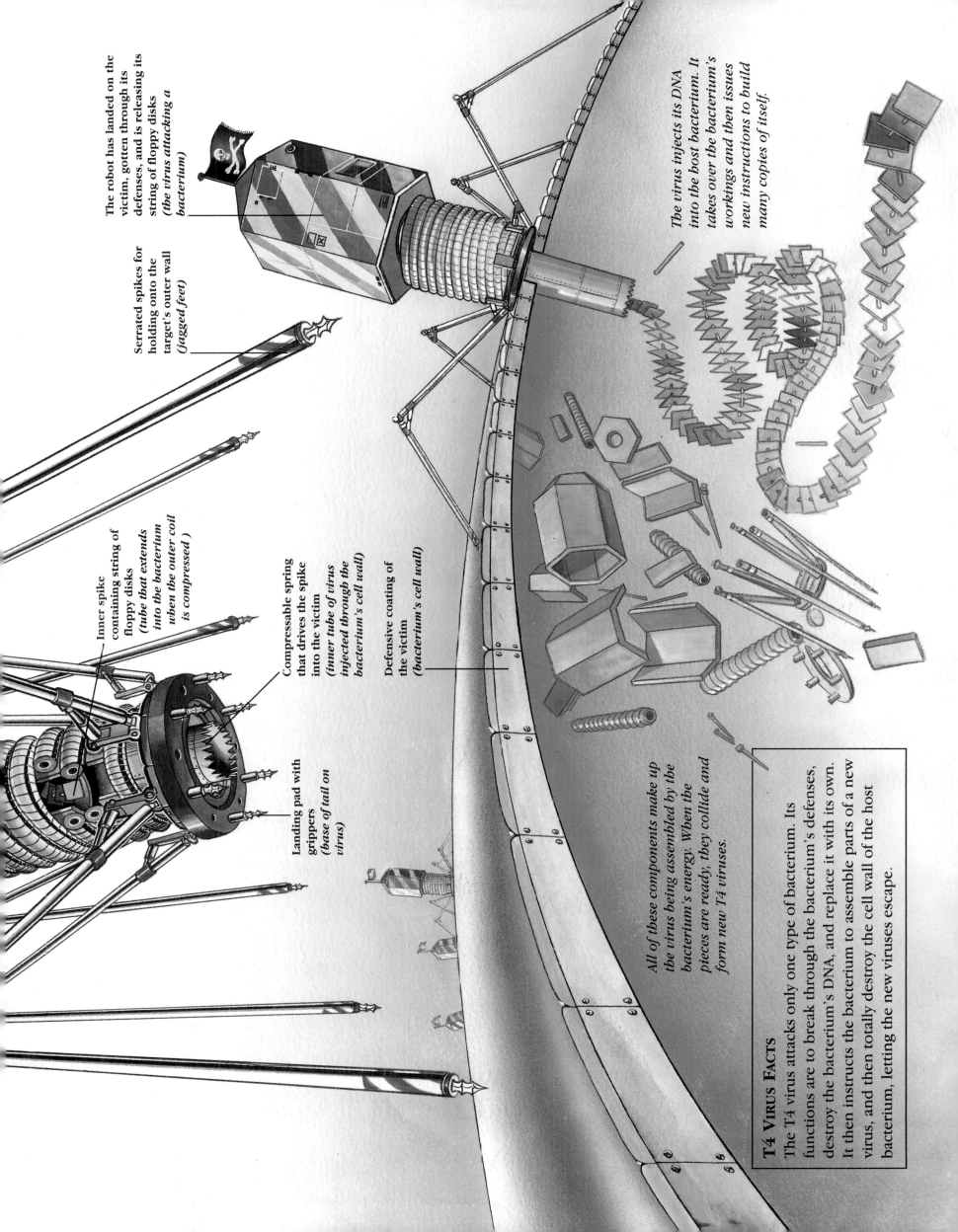

The robot has landed on the victim, gotten through its defenses, and is releasing its string of floppy disks (*the virus attacking a bacterium*)

Serrated spikes for holding onto the target's outer wall (*jagged feet*)

Inner spike containing string of floppy disks (*tube that extends into the bacterium when the outer coil is compressed*)

Compressable spring that drives the spike into the victim (*inner tube of virus injected through the bacterium's cell wall*)

Defensive coating of the victim (*bacterium's cell wall*)

Landing pad with grippers (*base of tail on virus*)

The virus injects its DNA into the host bacterium. It takes over the bacterium's workings and then issues new instructions to build many copies of itself.

All of these components make up the virus being assembled by the bacterium's energy. When the pieces are ready, they collide and form new T4 viruses.

T4 Virus Facts

The T4 virus attacks only one type of bacterium. Its functions are to break through the bacterium's defenses, destroy the bacterium's DNA, and replace it with its own. It then instructs the bacterium to assemble parts of a new virus, and then totally destroy the cell wall of the host bacterium, letting the new viruses escape.

GLOSSARY OF PARTS
Movement and Structure

All except the very smallest animals have bodies with some type of rigid skeleton. Movement occurs when muscles pull on the different parts of the skeleton. This happens when you walk, when a bird flies, or when an ant carries a seed to its nest. Vertebrate animals have a skeleton made of bones inside their bodies, while invertebrates, like insects, spiders, and crabs, have a hard outer covering called an exoskeleton supporting their bodies.

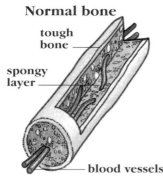

Normal bone
- tough bone
- spongy layer
- blood vessels

Stronger bone
- spongy layer
- tough bone
- blood vessels

Bones
All bones are made of a strong, rigid material. Each bone is a living organ with blood vessels in its center. Usually the outer layers of the bone are dense, while the center is more open and spongy. Where great support is needed, the outer layer is extra thick.

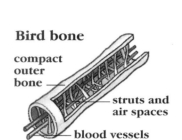

Bird bone
- compact outer bone
- struts and air spaces
- blood vessels

Bird bones
To fly, birds need light bodies. Their bones have a very thin outer layer. The inner spongy layer is made up of air-filled spaces between thin struts. This makes the bones very light.

Insect exoskeleton
The hard outer exoskeleton of an insect is called a cuticle. It is made of a horn-like material known as chitin. Each segment of an insect's body has a stiff cuticle, while the junctions between the segments are made of thinner, more flexible cuticle. Segments move when pairs of muscles that cross the junctions contract and release.

Insect leg

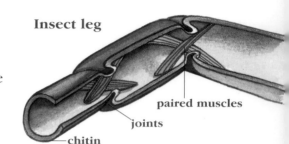
- paired muscles
- joints
- chitin

Hinges and joints
In vertebrates, joints are found where bones meet and movement occurs. Different joints allow different types and ranges of movement to happen.

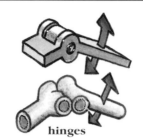
hinges

ball-and-socket

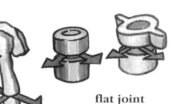
flat joint

Joints
The elbow joint is like a hinge, while the shoulder joint, which can move in many directions, is a ball-and-socket joint. Flat joints, like those between the vertebrae, allow only a small range of movement.

Vertebrae
The backbone of a vertebrate is made up of a chain of small bones called vertebrae that are linked together to allow bending. The robot vertebrae are constructed similarly. In the center of the vertebrae is a canal that contains the spinal cord (*see* senses and nerves).

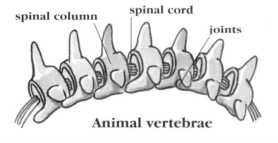
- spinal column
- spinal cord
- joints

Animal vertebrae

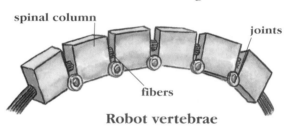
- spinal column
- joints
- fibers

Robot vertebrae

Muscles
Most animals move using muscles. Muscles are organs made of special fibers that have the power to contract (shorten by drawing together). When a muscle is stimulated by a nerve (*see* senses and nerves), it can change from a long, thin shape to a short, fat shape. Because the ends of the muscles are joined to different sections of the skeleton, the contracting muscles make the skeleton move. Some tubular organs, like the intestines, have layers of muscle fibers arranged in different directions. When these contract they cause food to pass through the organ.

Muscle fiber

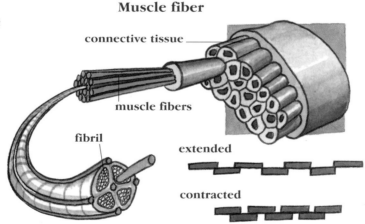
- connective tissue
- muscle fibers
- fibril
- extended
- contracted

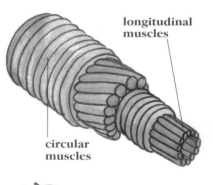
- longitudinal muscles
- circular muscles

Pistons
Muscles contract to move bones, whereas the pistons in the robots push out to cause movement. Each piston fits tightly inside a second tube. The space inside the tube is filled with fluid, usually a special oil. When fluid from a reservoir enters the tube, it forces the piston out because liquids cannot be squeezed or compressed.

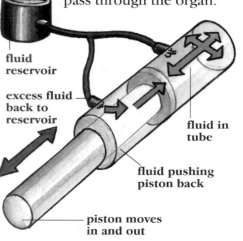
- fluid reservoir
- excess fluid back to reservoir
- fluid in tube
- fluid pushing piston back
- piston moves in and out

Muscular limbs
The tentacles of the giant squid have no bones. For movement, they use a system of longitudinal and circular muscles. The robot's system shows how these work. On one side of the tube the wires contract and squeeze the disks close together, pulling the tube in that direction. To straighten the tube out, wires contract on the opposite side.

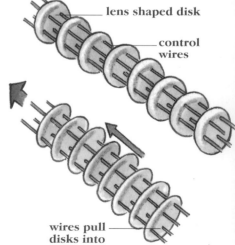
- lens shaped disk
- control wires
- wires pull disks into flatter shape

Feathers

Feathers are made of a tough substance called keratin. Each feather has a central shaft called a rachis from which extend thin side pieces called barbs. Tiny branches on the barbs, called barbules, allow the barbs to lock flexibly together and form the vanes of the feather. If the barbs of a vane split apart, all the bird has to do is pull the feather through its beak and the barbules will link together again.

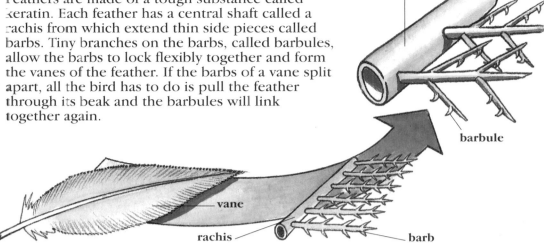

rachis

barbule

vane

rachis

barb

Scales

A reptile's scale consists of a flap of tough keratin. Between each scale and the next lies a more flexible, thinner layer of keratin. Together the scales act like chain-mail armor and protect the reptile. Under the keratin layer of the scales are pigment cells that give the reptile its color.

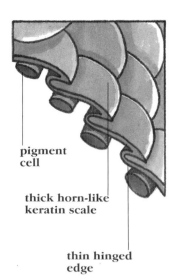

pigment cell

thick horn-like keratin scale

thin hinged edge

Senses and Nerves

Most animals control their actions with a nervous system made up of a brain and nerves that connect the brain to different parts of the body. The animal's senses receive and pass information about the outside world to the brain. The brain analyzes this data and sends messages to different parts of the body, causing them to react. The brain also has memory stores so that past experience can be used to influence future behavior. Most insects have no brain but instead have groups of nerve cells, called ganglia, that act in a similar way to a brain.

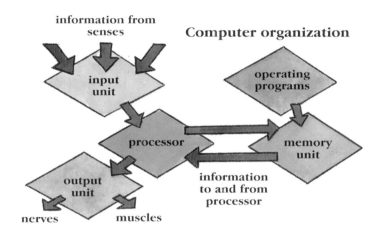

Computer organization

information from senses

input unit

operating programs

processor

memory unit

output unit

information to and from processor

nerves

muscles

Computers

The robots' brains are computers. Information is gathered from the sensors of the robots. Output signals travel along fibers to make parts of the robot work. The processing unit of the computer operates programs that are used to make decisions. The computer also has a large memory bank in which data is stored.

Nerves and cables

Signals in a nervous system and in a computer are both electrical. In a nervous system, the signals pass between nerve cells along paths called axons. In a computer, the signals consist of electrical currents that travel along very thin wires.

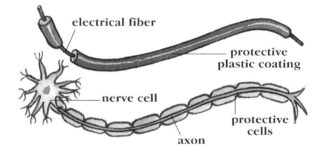

electrical fiber

protective plastic coating

nerve cell

axon

protective cells

Insect touch

The cuticle of an insect has sensory hairs extending from it. Each hair can bend at its base. If the hair senses something, it bends easily and a sensory cell sends an impulse to the ganglia. This is the basis for the insect's sense of touch.

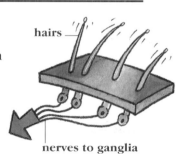

hairs

nerves to ganglia

Hearing and vibration sense

Animals usually have special sensory organs that allow them to receive sound waves. The system for hearing is similar in all animals. The sound waves hit a membrane which vibrates. Nerve cells connected to the membrane send signals to the brain that are interpreted as sound. Insects' ears can be anywhere on their body.

Ears and acoustic receptors

Land vertebrates have two ears. Sound makes the eardrum membrane, tiny bones, and fluid vibrate. A fish picks up vibrations through its lateral line. Sensory cells send messages to the fish's brain. An acoustic receptor in a robot does much the same thing, but it has a diaphragm that vibrates and passes signals on to an amplifier.

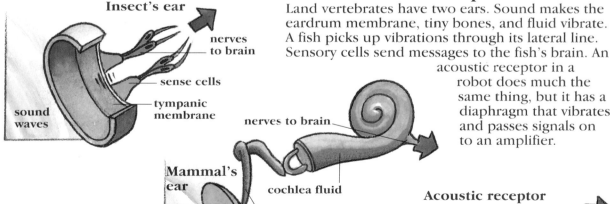

Insect's ear

nerves to brain

sense cells

tympanic membrane

sound waves

Mammal's ear

nerves to brain

cochlea fluid

ear bones

eardrum

sound waves

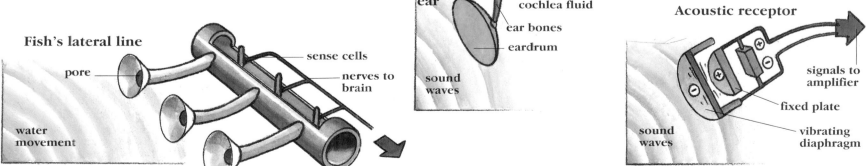

Fish's lateral line

pore

sense cells

nerves to brain

water movement

Acoustic receptor

signals to amplifier

fixed plate

vibrating diaphragm

sound waves

Seeing

Most animals have eyes. There are two major types of eyes. The one found in vertebrates is a fluid-filled sphere with a transparent window, or cornea, at the front. Light passes through the cornea and is focused by a lens to form an image on a light-sensitive surface called the retina. The retina is made up of millions of tiny light-sensitive cells called rods and cones. These convert the image on the retina into a pattern of nerve impulses that are sent to the brain to be interpreted.

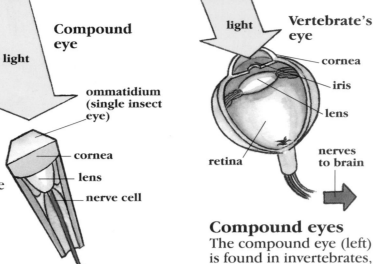

Compound eye

light

ommatidium (single insect eye)

cornea

lens

nerve cell

nerve to brain

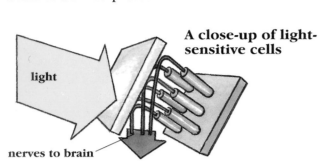

A close-up of light-sensitive cells

light

nerves to brain

Vertebrate's eye

light

cornea

iris

lens

retina

nerves to brain

Compound eyes

The compound eye (left) is found in invertebrates, such as insects. It is made up of hundreds, or even thousands, of tiny, telescope-like sensor units called ommatidia. Each of these responds to light that passes down its length.

Visual receptors

Visual receptors, like video cameras, have lens systems that focus an image on the back of a light-proof box. Sensory systems at the back of the box convert the image into electrical signals that transmit the image to the computer.

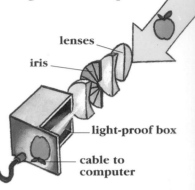

lenses

iris

light-proof box

cable to computer

Sense of smell

In the nasal passages of vertebrates are cells that respond to all sorts of chemical substances in the air. The nerve signals that these cells produce provide the animal with a sense of smell. Different cells recognize different scents. The clues that a sense of smell provides enable animals to find food, escape from predators, and find mates.

nasal passage

smell substances

air in nostril

throat

nerve signal to brain

sensory cells

Respiration and Digestion

Animals need a supply of energy. This comes from the food they eat. Food is digested and passed into the bloodstream as tiny particles of nutrients. These are then absorbed into cells. The nutrients are broken down when they combine with oxygen. When this breakdown (called internal respiration) happens, large amounts of energy are released.

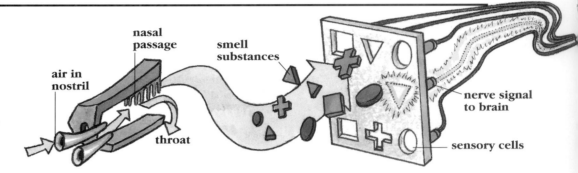

energy

nutrients

cell

water

oxygen

carbon dioxide

Breathing

For nutrient breakdown to occur, an animal needs a constant supply of oxygen. Land animals get their oxygen from the air. Animals that live underwater get oxygen from the water. Land and water animals breathe to get the oxygen, and the breathing is called external respiration.

membrane

oxygen

blood vessel

Lung

vein

artery

bronchi

alveoli

carbon dioxide moves out from blood

Alveolus

membrane

oxygen moves from air to blood

oxygen-rich air in

carbon dioxide out

Lungs

Land animals pull oxygen into their lungs by breathing. The inner lining of the lungs is a huge, moist surface covered with tiny blood vessels called capillaries. Blood passing through these vessels picks up the oxygen as it travels across the very thin membrane that divides the air from the blood (far left).

Other types

Insects and fish have a wide variety of oxygen-gathering organs. Most of the aquatic animals have gills. Water flows across gills so that the blood vessels inside can pick up oxygen. Insects and spiders have a series of tubes that lead to the inner respiratory organs.

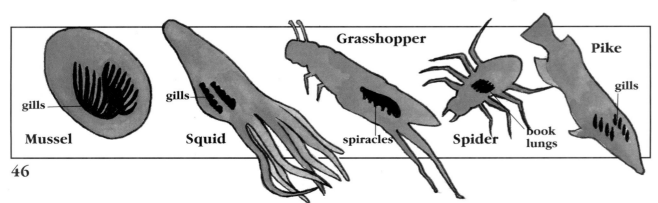

gills

Mussel

gills

Squid

Grasshopper

spiracles

Spider

book lungs

Pike

gills

gills

Blood supply

Blood is a body fluid that performs many functions. It carries oxygen and nutrients to all of the body cells so that they can carry out internal respiration. It removes waste substances like carbon dioxide and urea from the body cells and carries them to the lungs and kidneys to be expelled. It also carries hormones around the body. Hormones are special substances that control some of the body's activities. The hormone insulin, for example, controls the levels of sugars in the blood.

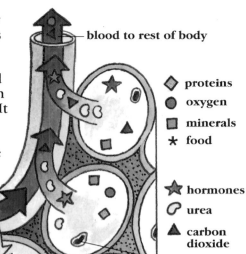

blood to rest of body

◇ proteins
● oxygen
■ minerals
✳ food

⭐ hormones
𝒸 urea
▲ carbon dioxide

cell nucleus

Simple hearts

A heart is a muscle in the system of tubes—blood vessels—that passes blood around an animal's body. By pumping, the heart pushes blood through the body. This pumping action is caused by muscles in the wall of the heart. In insects and mollusks, the heart is not much more than thickened blood vessels. Muscles squeeze around the vessels to force blood through the body.

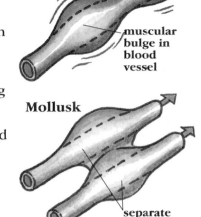

Insect

muscular bulge in blood vessel

Mollusk

separate chambers

Pumps

The hearts of animals use muscles to push blood through the vessels in the blood system. In the robots, a variety of pumping machines are used to move body fluids. The rotor pump (left) uses spinning rotor blades to push the fluid through an outlet tube.

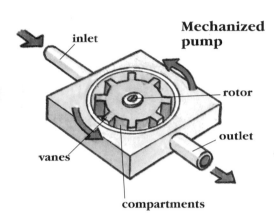

Mechanized pump

inlet

rotor

outlet

vanes

compartments

Circulation

In insects, blood travels from the heart to the body where it picks up oxygen. In fish, blood circulates from the heart to the gills, through the body, and back to the heart. In land vertebrates, blood travels from the heart to the lungs, back to the heart, and then into the body before returning to the heart.

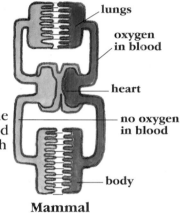

Insect

heart

open body cavity

Fish

body

gills

heart

lungs

oxygen in blood

heart

no oxygen in blood

body

Mammal

Digestion

This is the chemical process that breaks food down into nutrients, which the body uses for energy. Digestion begins when food is chewed by the teeth. The process continues with the help of digestive enzymes. These substances break down particles of food into smaller ones that can be absorbed by cells. Proteins are turned into amino acids, starches into sugars, and fats into fatty acids.

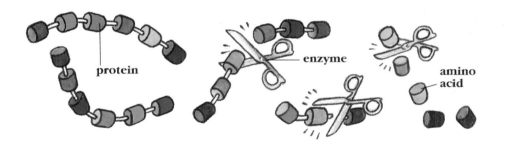

protein

enzyme

amino acid

The process

All except a few tiny animals have an intestine. Food is first mixed with saliva in the mouth, which lubricates its passage and adds digestive enzymes. These begin to break the food down. In the stomach, acid that kills bacteria is added, and more digestive enzymes are secreted from the stomach wall. In the intestines, additional enzymes from the pancreas and liver continue the process of digestion. The nutrients that are produced are absorbed through the wall of the intestine. The final sections of the intestine remove excess water from the material that remains. This waste, called feces, is then expelled through the anus.

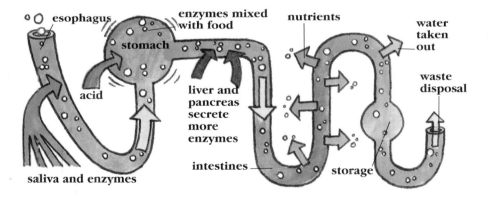

esophagus

enzymes mixed with food

stomach

nutrients

water taken out

acid

liver and pancreas secrete more enzymes

waste disposal

intestines

storage

saliva and enzymes

Digestive organs

Most animals have similar digestive organs. While they use the same process as described above, there are some differences. The giraffe has a stomach with four chambers that help digest grass; the bird, grasshopper, and chameleon have food storage areas called crops; and the mussel has a mouth inside its shell that collects food particles gathered by its gills.

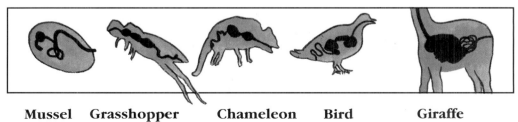

Mussel   Grasshopper   Chameleon   Bird   Giraffe

Index

The numbers in *italics* refer to illustrations of the real animals.

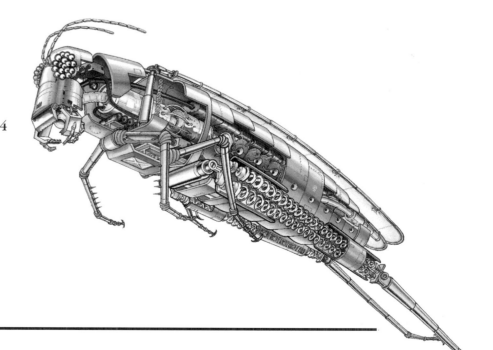

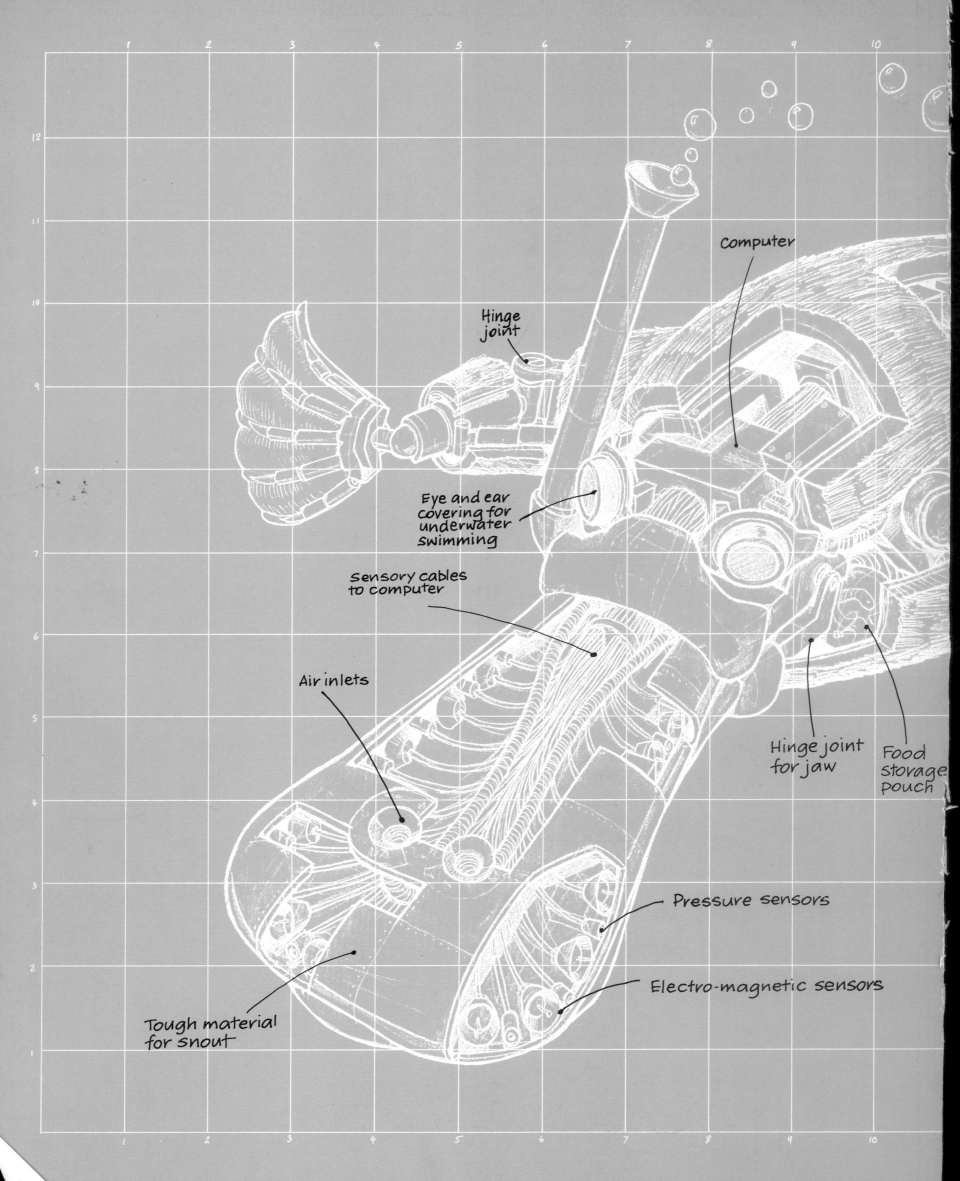

Computer

Hinge joint

Eye and ear covering for underwater swimming

Sensory cables to computer

Air inlets

Hinge joint for jaw

Food storage pouch

Tough material for snout

Pressure sensors

Electro-magnetic sensors